BOROUGH OF KEIGHLEY
PUBLIC LIBRARIES

REFERENCE LIBRARY

Book No.	Class No.
17166	796.6

CYCLING'S 'CIRCUS'

Cycling's 'Circus'

CHAS MESSENGER

PELHAM BOOKS

First published in Great Britain by
PELHAM BOOKS LTD
52 Bedford Square
London, W.C.1
1971

W
£1·75

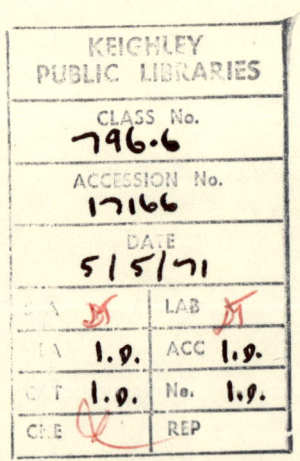
7207 0490 1

Set and printed in Great Britain by
Tonbridge Printers Ltd, Peach Hall Works,
Tonbridge, Kent, in Times ten on twelve point, on
paper supplied by P. F. Bingham Ltd, and bound by
James Burn at Esher, Surrey

INTRODUCTION

. . . a 'Tour' is pure 'Circus' and, who amongst us can go to a Circus and not be thrilled . . . a 'Tour' is a challenge to a bike rider, an academic exercise to pit his craft, his years of knowledge, his courage and determination, against the winning of not one race, but many races in a given number of days . . . after all, you would have to be pretty insensitive to the sight of so much sweat, toil and tears in

CYCLING'S CIRCUS

CHAS MESSENGER

CONTENTS

1 OVERTURE TO THE 'CIRCUS'   11

2 THE 'HARD LUCK' TOUR   17
   Tour of Britain, 1951. August 19th – September 1st

3 THE 'LONER'S' TOUR   38
   Tour of Britain, 1952. August 22nd – September 6th

4 THE 'FIGHTING' TOUR   60
   Tour of Britain, 1953. September 6th – 19th

5 THE 'TOUR DE TAMBURLINI'   79
   Tour of Britain, 1954. June 6th – 19th

6 THE 'HOLIDAY CAMP' TOUR   99
   Tour of Britain, 1955. September 3rd – 10th

7 THE BAILES 'RUMBLE'   113
   Circuit of Britain, 1954. August 14th – 23rd

8 PURE 'CIRCUS'   129
   Circuit of Britain, 1955. July 15th – 23rd

9 OVER THE 'BROWN'   147
   Circuit of Britain, 1956. August 11th – 18th

RACE RESULTS   170

INDEX   179

ILLUSTRATIONS

facing page

1 Incident at Newhaven during 1951 Tour   32

2 The field hammering through Newmarket   32

3 Eugene Garnier of France   33

4 Jimmy Saville   33

5 Ken Russell during the 1952 Tour   64

6 Bev Wood during the 1953 Tour   64

7 The 1952 Tour riders on their first hill prime   65

8 Gordon Thomas, winner of 1953 Tour   72

9 At Ripon, on Stage 4, 1954 Tour   72

10 Ken Russell leading in 1955 Tour   73

11 Eugene Tamburlini, winner of 1954 Tour   88

12 Tamburlini wearing 'Yellow Jersey'   89

13 Bob Maitland, 1955 Tour   89

14 Lead group on climb of the Brecons, 1955 Circuit   96

15 Viv Bailes, 1954 Circuit winner   96

16 Raymond Holliday, 1955 Circuit   97

Illustrations

17 Desmond Robinson on Stage 4, 1955 Circuit   128

18 Brian Haskell, having to walk, during 1955 Circuit   128

19 Gil Taylor, stage 2, 1956 Circuit   129

20 Timekeepers and judges viewing finish of 1956   129
Circuit at Worthing

*Thanks are due to the following for permission
to reproduce photographs in which they hold
copyright: London Express, 1, 2, 5, 7; Cycling,
3, 8, 9, 10, 11, 13, 14, 15, 17, 20; John Otway, 4,
Temple Press, 6, 18, 19*

MAPS

DRAWN BY JOE MANGAN

Tour of Britain, 1951   26

Tour of Britain, 1952   50

Tour of Britain, 1953   68

Tour of Britain, 1954   89

Tour of Britain, 1955   107

Circuit of Britain, 1954   121

Circuit of Britain, 1955   137

Circuit of Britain, 1956   159

1: *Overture to the 'Circus'*

Cycle racing, any type of cycle-racing, is an eye-catcher, for not only is colour the keynote, but there is the thrill of speed and the graceful rhythm of tough athletic endeavour. All combine to make up a spectacle which can hold even the non-expert eye, as well as that of the most knowledgeable. But a 'Tour' (stage-racing) is a special part of the sport, and it is the *only* big sporting event where the participants *go to their audience*!

To my mind, a 'Tour' is pure 'Circus' and, who amongst us can go to a Circus and not be thrilled?

Ringside seats are there for anyone who cares to walk up, and they will have nothing to pay. The 'Tour' has its own parade of decorated vehicles, and the 'oom-pa-pa' is provided by the elaborate publicity vehicles with their loudspeaker equipment. The performers in our 'Circus' are the officials, the competitors, the team managers, the mechanics, the publicity and press men. The ring-masters are the officials; the property men, the team managers and mechanics; the ballyhoo men the publicity and press men.

The clowns and acrobats are the riders in their colourful costumes, enhanced by the glitter of their dazzling machines; the lights of the television cameras; the flash bulbs of the press photographers.

As the 'merry-go-round' speeds up, so brash music blares out over the speaker system at starts and finishes; the announcers (barkers) lose their voices as they croak out the virtues, performances and life-stories of the competitors; the shouts and cries of vendors of newspapers; ice-cream; pop-corn; cowboy hats and the like add to the din, and you can virtually smell the sawdust and naphtha as you push through the milling throng.

After all, anyone, anywhere, would have to be pretty insensitive not to be moved by the sight of up to 80 riders in colourful jerseys, sweating it out at an average speed of 25 and more miles per hour;

11

pedalling up steep hills and over towering mountains on which even the official cars sometimes stall, and suffering untold agonies not only for mile after mile, but for day after day.

So completely *different* is 'le Tour' (stage-racing) from single day racing that a rider can never really be termed a complete bike rider until he has ridden a 'Tour' of seven, or more, stages.

For a single day race, the preparation is really of the simplest, and provided that the rider remembers to take with him everything that he needs, the event is not fraught with too many anxieties. But preparation for a 'Tour' is entirely another thing, both for officials as well as riders.

A 'Tour' abroad can be a nightmare, from many points of view, for once there you can't just ring home for any bits and pieces you may have forgotten. Excess baggage is always a problem and there is the classic story of a British National team who went out of this country on a fifteen day 'Tour' abroad and, so tight was money in those days that they carried most of the mechanics' tools about their person, besides wearing several vests, jerseys and jumpers each to boot!

Even a 'Tour' in this country can have its problems. Not only does the rider have to remember to pack three of this; four of that; two of those *and,* don't forget your crash-helmet . . . but any fads and fancies he may have, food wise, have to be catered for, for you must remember that this highly trained athlete has to cart everything around in a suitcase out of which he virtually lives for the entire 'Tour'.

It's true that he doesn't live in a caravan like a true circus performer, but he certainly leads a thoroughly roving existence.

Please, do not be misled by the word 'Tour', for the word, used in cycle-racing, does not mean, in any way, the leisurely, delightfully free ambling around the countryside enjoyed by the cycle tourist. In the French racing vocabulary, it means a race of exceptional toughness and duration.

The world-famous 'Tour de France' is legendary. It is a race for professionals; a race of tremendous bally-hoo and publicity impact, that tests out the greatest roadmen in the world over its 3,000 miles of route each year, and which include mountain passes of many thousands of feet.

To ride in such a 'Tour' is a dream that comes to few.

Overture to the 'Circus'

A 'Tour' is made up of a number of daily stages, each stage really being a race in itself, often with *Prime* prizes on the way, sometimes in towns, but more often on the lofty heights of a mountain summit, and prizes for the leaders at the stage finish. According to how the 'Tour' is run, the leading riders (up to six) are awarded time bonuses, and these are deducted from the total time.

There is also a 'King of the Mountains' section, where points are awarded for the first men over the top of mountain passes, and also a Team section, where the time of the first three men of a team, on each day's racing is added together. The rider with the lowest 'total' time, after all bonuses are deducted, and time penalties added is the 'Race Leader', and he wears the coveted *Maillot Jaune*, or yellow jersey.

Riders wear distinctive team jerseys so that they are easily recognisable to rivals, officials and public alike, but only one man can wear the *maillot jaune* of the 'Race Leader'. He is always a marked man. He is the rider who is nursed by his team-mates. As for the rest, it is their job to do everything to beat the yellow-jerseyed rider by as many seconds or minutes as they can, and so endeavour to take the *maillot jaune* from him.

Food is carried by the riders in special pockets of their jerseys, and a wide and varied knowledge is necessary to feed them. The food must be easily digestible and, at the same time, be energy giving. Thinly cut bread, butter and honey sandwiches; sultanas; sugar lumps; glucose sweets; fruit of all description form part of each riders private 'tuck box'. In many 'Tours' they are handed up to him in a food bag – known to the cycle-racing fraternity as a 'musette'.

A 'Tour' is a challenge to a rider; an academic exercise to pit his craft, his years of knowledge, his courage and determination, against the winning of, not one race, but many races in a given number of days. This is not so much a race as a cavalcade of energy, skill and enthusiasm. To summon the skill, determination and stamina, and to keep it for the duration of the 'Tour', is just to provide the basic requirements in a long drawn tactical battle that goes on for every minute of the race.

Many times during the race they will be too pent up to sleep. and many is the hour that will be spent tossing and turning, reliving the events of the day, or wrestling with the problems of the morrow.

A stage, any stage, starts at the crack of dawn, when the route-markers go out, and does not end until very late at night, or even the following morning. A 'Tour' needs many officials; Organisers; Commissaires; Judges; Timekeepers; Mobile Marshals; Feeding Managers; Team Managers; Mechanics: Service Personnel, etc. etc., to complete a whole team that has to keep 'the Circus' on the road, and the team never stops working for the whole time of the race.

It is probable that a civic dignitary will lower the flag to start the day's racing but all events in this country are neutralised until it is considered safe for them to start racing, and then they are let go. Out in front go the mobile marshals, and it is their job to watch for and marshal bad corners, obstructions, etc., and to advise race officials if there is a traffic jam ahead, or perhaps straying sheep and cattle on some of the wilder stretches of the course.

Attacks—attempts to get away from the rest, are made where the hazards are hardest: at a tricky bend; on a hill or mountain climb; on a fast run downhill, or into a head wind. First one man and then another will dictate the tempo of the race and if a break is made the endeavour will be for the riders to get as far away as possible, possibly with one of his team-mates. As a break gathers speed it will be noticed that rivals will take turns in pacing one another. This is a tactical move to ensure that only those few riders in the break will fight out the stage but, in the final sprint for the line, the rivalry will reassert itself. Meanwhile, back in the bunch, or field, team-mates are doing all they can to slow the rest of the riders.

For a rider in the break there is always the fear of being caught; the fear that his strength will be over-taxed and he will 'sell-out'; the gnawing pangs of hunger when the man next to you has plenty and you daren't ask for any, for fear that he'll realise that you've 'had it', and, if you have ever been away with a leading group for hours, and there is still plenty of miles to do, the growing feeling of tiredness gradually descends through your body and down through your legs to your feet, and then the meaning of being in 'a break' smacks you straight in the face.

14

When a strong wind blows across the road, the whole field will 'echelon' out until a long 'snake' can be seen for hundreds of yards. Gradually, the pace at the front will increase; gradually, the tail of the 'snake' will commence to waggle until finally, in one's and two's, the 'not so fit' commence to get dropped off and the field gradually dwindles, getting smaller and smaller, until finally, only the 'giants' are left to pound out their hearts and get ahead of the field and perhaps be the first man home for the day.

Comes the quiet of the hills and mountains, and to the 'Tour' rider they just mean a job of work. The stillness is broken only by the whirr of wheels, but on every rider the muscles stand out with effort, as he batters himself against the obstacle ahead. What a climb this is! Fantastic corners, nurtured by nature out of the grim rock surface, reaching up with hungry hands. Up and up they climb, like glowing birds, across a rough patch that brings hearts into mouths in case of puncture and round the last hair-pin bend to the black-rimmed top of the mountain.

Then comes the long, long sweep down, round bends that disappear from view, where the slightest slip means a drop of hundreds of feet to the rocks below. You are moving fast, but others are moving faster. Brakes will get hot, the rubber will wear fast. Water tinkles merrily alongside the road, but all you can think of is that No. 49 has gained a couple of hundred yards on you!

Along the valley, the brown waters swirl and snarl their way onwards. Comes another climb and the riders grind their way up into the vastness stretching away. The 'break' has long since gone, and all we have to look at is road. On and on they ride, over a switch-back of a road, until the finish comes into sight and another day is complete.

Nowadays, so many riders have 'Toured', both at home and abroad, that the newcomer will be able to learn from the vast amount of knowledge that has been accumulated over the years; get lists of do's and don'ts, be told of major snags, etc., which in 'Tours' long since gone, cropped up time and time again, but are now very much a thing of the past.

The 'Tour' rider today has the path very much smoothed for him and this, of course, is how it should be, for a courier having to race over seven days or more should have all the little, and big problems of what, how, why and when, smoothed out for

15

him, so that his only and complete worry is to get on the bike each day and race.

This was not so in the 'good old days'. Preparation for a stage race was virtually unknown and had to be learnt the hard, hard way, by bitter experience. Equipment used then, and made to do, would probably be laughed at by even the merest junior today, but the rider then had no choice.

With so little experience, and ofttimes with very inferior equipment, some of these couriers were real 'toughies' and put up fantastic performances over courses and terrain that had never been seen the like of before. The accounts of these past 'Circuses' are a tribute to their valour in the field, and to the British League of Racing Cyclists for having the tenacity, the courage, and the audacity in the face of so much opposition, of putting them on.

Perhaps it might be said that these were the halcyon days of road-racing in this country, and it is hoped that their memory will be perpetuated within these pages.

2: The 'Hard Luck' Tour

Tour of Britain, 1951

August 19th—September 1st

It really all began way back in 1942 when Percy Stallard, ever a one for sticking his neck out, pushed the road-racing boat out, and the Wolverhampton-Llangollen was the first road race of hundreds of thousands that have since been run.

Of course, he was suspended by the National Cyclists Union, but this only added a fillip to the more 'hot under the collar' rebels, and the whole erupted, becoming white hot in debate and, before the year was out, the British League of Racing Cyclists came into being and the struggle was on!

The 'few' grew and, by 1943, when the first stage of three days was held in Kent, there was a sharp nucleus of riders that spurred on the thoughts of many more, and the dividing line between the Union and the League got noticeably bigger.

The League built up its strength, not on the bones of the Union, but in its own infallibility to produce what was wanted – road racing. They were tough, hard fought, halcyon days, but they produced events like the marathon Brighton-to-Glasgow's. Events in which riders rode themselves into the ground, got up, and then went round the town looking for the cheapest lodgings they could find, or even slept in the hedge. Money was tight, but tight, but the League, and its members, never faltered, they just kept on going when every odd was against them.

It was left to 'odd job man', Doug Peakall to start co-ordinating stage events, and this live-wire of a man, who was with the Union when the League came into being, was out in Italy during the war, forming a club out there and noting ideas on stage-racing that were to be used to advantage when he returned to this country and joined up with the League. It was 1949 before he organised the six-day Brighton to Glasgow, but he was already ferreting around for a more ambitious event.

His foresight and tenacity brought fruition in 1951, Festival of Britain year. The *Daily Express* undertook the complete sponsorship of a 14-day race and put up £1,000 in prize money. This was double anything the League had had before and the Union were soon snapping at their heels, trying to cut out the gravy.

Things like a 1,400 miles cycle race just don't 'happen'. It takes months of hard work, and the only data they had to go on, and to hand, were their own efforts on the six-day events – a vastly different kettle of fish.

Nothing so tough, so flamboyant, so gratifying, had ever been attempted in this country before yet such was the mood of cyclists of the day that it was only the road-racing adherents who applauded what was an audacious sporting triumph.

The rebel League was harassed on every turn by the Union, yet Doug Peakall got his international riders from France, Ireland and Scotland to the assembly at the 'Cock Pit' in Hyde Park, London, on 15th August, 1951, and the total of 49 starters was made up with teams from British 'equipes', Dayton; I.T.P.; Viking; Gnutti and Pennine, all, except Viking, now sadly gone, making up the rest with Regional *amateur* teams.

The French team, also rebels in their own right, were a bit 'long in the tooth' age-wise, compared to our riders, but they had quite a list of successes to their credit, while the Irish riders, rebels too, were about to taste their first long stage race.

The bug eyes of television and film cameras were taking in all the details. The sun shone, men massaged legs, put food into pockets, and whiled away the few moments left of freedom. At 9.30 a.m., they rose, put legs over machines and, by 9.45 a.m. they were trundling out of Hyde Park en-route for the 'Start' proper on Farnborough Common in Kent.

A leisurely lunch, then outside for a breath of air . . . and there were two minutes to go!

STAGE 1. LONDON – HASTINGS – BRIGHTON 83 MILES.

Such was the publicity in the *Express* that there were thousands out on the route and, as the small colourful group line up ready for the 'off', such was the chatter that the announcer could not make himself heard, and the flag went down for a ragged start, right on the dot of noon.

Down, into Sevenoaks, and along the humpty backs to Tonbridge. Feelers are put out, but no-one attempted to bite. The front of the bunch jockeyed back and forth, and the hill out of Tonbridge produces a long-drawn-out-line, but everyone was in the bunch at the top.

On the undulating run down to Hastings, one or two came out of the back, notably Jimmy Saville (now disc-jockey extraordinary), and the strong tang of the salt sea air did not produce energy enough for the stragglers to get back on. Ian Steel (Viking) and Len West became fed up with the inactivity and disappeared, taking with them Laurent of France. They bludgeoned their way along, but Laurent kept on leaving gaps which they had to fill, and at 60 miles they were just one big un-happy family!

They had just about enough time to catch their breath and up came East Dean Hill. Short, it's true, but with gradients of 1 in 7, it was just made for a breakaway and Gabriel Audemard of France swung out from the bunch, hunched over his handlebars and was away, shouting to Edmond Pierre as he went past. At the top, he had seconds to spare, and Pierre was coming up too, but bringing young Mick Howarth with him.

The swinging lanes helped Audemard, and he reached Newhaven first, but found the level-crossing gate closed. He jumped off the machine and, allowing an official to carry his bike, races over the footbridge and as he jumped on his bike once more, Pierre, who had given Howarth a 'real lacing' reached the crossing, fifteen precious seconds in front of the rest.

A lively bunch reached the level-crossing together and it was a bit of cyclo-cross for all concerned before riding off towards Brighton. Across the rolling Downs of Rottingdean, Pierre could see his compatriot, Audemard, but could not catch him, and with these two it was 'out of sight, out of mind', for the rest have disintegrated along the way. The Irish had mechanical trouble, but were still churning 'em round, and the tail is wagging over a long distance.

Down on to the Madeira Drive hurtled Audemard, and twenty thousand people cheered themselves hoarse as he crossed the line, to be followed by Pierre only nine seconds later. Next came Alec Taylor (Gnutti), and the rest hobbled in in ones and twos.

France had taken the first stage, and the team race, despite a 30 second penalty on Audemard for letting his bike be carried across the footbridge, but the other teams did not seem to be particularly worried.

It had been a 'bitty' first stage, but one that had sparked off the imagination of the general public and the sponsors seemed satisfied with the publicity. Forty-nine finished the stage and went off to sleep, the sleep of the righteous, with probably bad dreams of the next day's stage.

STAGE 2. BRIGHTON TO BOURNEMOUTH 95 MILES.

The jerseys, the shining bicycles, the foreign gestures and grimaces all go to create an atmosphere that comes from a big sporting event. Things get sorted out eventually and they lined-up to ribald comments from mates not in the race, to last minute instructions from team managers, mechanics, and anyone else who cared to give advice.

Out in front went a car and the riders followed it through the neutralised area, along the front at Brighton and Hove, and out to Old Shoreham. At the Toll Bridge, straps were tightened, the flag dropped and away they go with the speed mounting up, mile by mile.

It was at Arundel, just as they swung round in the shadow of the Castle, that a dozen or so crept off the front, and there is a break. Pierre was there, but so was Parker, Buttle and Scales of the Dayton team. They worked hard, taking turn and turn about and the lead increased slowly but surely, and at 45 miles, near to Portsdown Hill they had a lead of nearly 3 minutes.

Just about here, Dave Bedwell (Dayton) jumped the bunch and, pounding out a rhythm that was not to be denied, gradually hauled back the leaders and finally became one of them himself. Now Dayton had four men in the break!

Down in the New Forest something stirred and, at Stoney Cross, came the first *prime* hill of the race. The bonus was half-a-minute in time and Pierre went flat out to take it, leaving behind a startled foursome. Tiny Bedwell hunched over his machine and gave chase and coming from 'out of nowhere' took the Frenchman just before the summit, getting the first points in the 'King of the Mountain' trophy.

Thousands were out along the route cheering the riders on their way, and cars, coaches and lorries pulled off the road to give the riders a clear run. The Irish still had their run of bad luck tagging along behind them, and all of them had had trouble with their gears.

From the 'Cross, the Dayton men were for ever on the alert. First Pierre tried a long one, and a Dayton rider pulled him back. Time and again this happened and on and on they went, trying tactics that until then had been unheard of, and still the Dayton men were in there, 'pulling them back', but more have come up to swell the lead bunch.

Very soon they were into Bournemouth and all sit up to ease aching backs, tighten toe-straps and look over the opposition. Fifteen riders turned as one, into Kings Park, and the charade begins as first one, and then another put his front wheel in front to take the lead, while all about him dancing bods are gyrating like puppets on a string.

It was Don Wilson who finally broke clear, with the attendant Bedwell on his wheel and, at 20 yards to go, Dave goes like a shot from a gun, and gets the verdict by three lengths from Don Wilson, with Johnny Hibell at inches, and the other twelve sweating lads, breathing down the back of his neck.

Little groups come in, some with tales of woe and trouble, but 39 are 'home and dry' only 11 minutes after the leaders, and this augurs well for the rest of the race. The local organisers have done a magnificent job here and there were few complaints on organisation.

The service van of Cyclo Gear Co. under Harold Martin was working flat-out within minutes of the finish, bringing up to scratch any gears or mechanical defect that might lose a rider those precious seconds on the next day's stage, and they were to go on working far into the night.

Edmund Pierre, France, 37 years old, was now the holder of the *maillot jaune*, but the French team had dropped to fourth place behind, Dayton, I.T.P. and the Viking men.

STAGE 3. BOURNEMOUTH TO PLYMOUTH 122 MILES.

Around Bournemouth's Pavilion Forecourt milled thousands of spectators watching the colourful cavalcade as it made its preparations for the day's sport. Last minute adjustments were made to brakes and gears; legs, arms and chests massaged as the greying sky showed signs of there being heavy rain.

Just outside Poole, the rains came and were to continue almost non-stop throughout the day. They negotiated the tricky corners leading to Dorchester and the main bunch remained in one tight, compact heap.

On the climb through Dorchester, Audemard went into the attack. In short, sharp hops he took off, and it was left to Trev. Fenwick (Pennine) and Don Wilson to chase him, and the most phenomenal 'bit and bit' started in earnest. 5 miles from Dorchester another small group caught them, including Ian Steel and Mike Eastwood. Steel went straight to the front, and off the front, all in one movement, but Audemard went with him. It was only Eastwood who saw the danger, and he whipped smartly down the ranks, across to the other side of the road and was gone.

Rapidly the three drew away and by the time Axminster was reached with just over half the course completed, they had a lead of over 5 minutes. At Haldon Hill, Steel shot through smartly on his turn and at the top had a fifty yard lead on the Frenchman. They waited for Eastwood, but he was tiring visibly and although they sped on at cracking pace, he was just a passenger, and it was obvious to all that Mike's miles were numbered.

At 90 miles he blew and the shattered hulk was left behind. It was now Steel and Audemard with 30 miles still to cover. Steel made all the running 'cos the Frenchman just wouldn't go to the front. He used Steel as a windshield, and on the undulations through Ashburton, Buckfastleigh and Ivybridge took every advantage.

Back in the bunch, Bedwell had got restless and attacked,

attacked and attacked. He was brought back time after time, for Pierre was with the group and shouldered his fair share of the work of slowing up 'Iron Man' Bedwell.

As the leading pair slithered their way into Plymouth, it was Ian Steel who took the initiative and sprinted even harder, taking Audemard by surprise and beating him to the line by 3 lengths. Four minutes, thirty-five seconds later it was the tiny Bedwell who took third place, leaving the rest standing with a 100 yards to go. This gave him a 30 second bonus and he took the lead on General Classification, with 4 seconds to spare over the Frenchman, Pierre, and became the first British holder of the *maillot jaune*.

STAGE 4. PLYMOUTH TO WESTON SUPER MARE 103 MILES.

The yellow jersey supplied by the organisers didn't fit 'rolypoly' Bedwell very well, and it looked as though a tuck in it would have done it the world of good. The ceremonial send-off was something worth seeing, and out of Plymouth they rode, back the way they had come the previous day, and all was well with the bunch until near Exeter.

Suddenly, Frank Seel (I.T.P.) right at the back of the bunch, punctured. Ken Jowett, a team-mate saw his plight and stopped with him. The tyre proved to be 'one of those' and rapidly the bunch went out of sight. After a couple of minutes had gone by they still hadn't got the tyre off, and they were in dead trouble.

Up front, Ken Russell suddenly missed them, and turned round, calling to Geoff. Clarke and they both turned round and rode back. The tyre was at last replaced and the bunch were at five minutes. The I.T.P. men got down to it, doing a team pursuit that nearly set the road alight, and eight miles further on they had made it back to the bunch.

The heaving, struggling mass sped through town and village, up hill, down dale, and no one was attempting to get away. Haldon Hill was in sight and it was Bedwell, the mighty, who 'led out'. Rider after rider jockeyed for position, but it was the 'Iron man' who sped across the line first to notch up more points in the 'King of the Mountains', and earn himself another half minute bonus.

Down they hurtled, at something over 50 m.p.h. displaying

fantastic skill in controlling their machines. At the bottom, four had gone with the wind, in Laurent, McCarthy, Welch and Addie, and were really setting a pace that had the others banging on their ears. Groups formed and disintegrated and back in the main bunch were Bedwell and Pierre.

On to the Exeter By-pass and it was every man for himself. Like an arrow Bedwell shot out of the middle of the bunch, with Greenfield glued to his wheel. They became two tiny specks in the distance before anyone took up the chase, and it was all over. In less than five miles they caught and passed the two intermediate groups and were up with the leaders. Pierre, sadly, but unwisely had missed his chance when Bedwell had attacked, and was still back in the main bunch.

The only French rider there, Laurent, took a beating as the speed got faster and faster, and a short, sharp rise saw him 'off the back' and that left ten jolly 'grimpeurs' to soldier on at a steady 30 m.p.h. Joe Lennon from Ireland suddenly found that a couple of cogs on his freewheel were missing, and Addie suffered the pangs of stomach cramp, and then there were eight.

Over the Bridgwater flats they kept hard at it for the finish was almost in sight. On the chicane on to the Promenade, Bedwell held the pole line and anyone who wanted to win had to get round him. It's a long, long straight, about ¾ mile up to the finish and, in line abreast they hammered it out, fighting wheel to wheel, with the Bedwell 'burst' getting the verdict by 1½ lengths from Wilson, with Derek Buttle at a wheel. Pierre trundled in just under 3 minutes later and dropped to fourth place on General Classification.

They 'rested' in Weston the next day, some going out and doing an hour's steady riding, while other's desported themselves on the beach, lending glamour to the whole with donkey-races, or a bit of sky-larking before taking it easy.

STAGE 5. CARDIFF TO WOLVERHAMPTON 112 MILES.

It was raining again as the riders made their way on to the boat that was to take them across the Bristol Channel, and 'The Duke' (Jimmy Saville) missed the boat and had a hair-raising journey by car to the Start.

24

From the City Hall in Cardiff, the wind was right behind, and the 46 riders left in had decided to make the most of it. At Newport, the field was already split and the struggle was on in earnest. Les Scales took the Wales into England *prime*, but only by inches. The bunch became one compact mass and no one was allowed to get away.

50 miles went by just before Hereford, and Seel, Bill Bellamy and Ian Steel shot round a corner and by the time they passed through the town, had a lead of 30 seconds. The bunch screamed after them and, in 5 miles, back they came.

Don Wilson took the lead, and just then disaster struck. There was a three vehicle smash-up between a hospital utility, a private car and a fuel lorry, and one of the doors smacked Wilson straight in the chest and knocked him off his machine.

As one man, the whole field stopped, refusing to continue until Wilson was patched up, and unofficial observers say it was in the region of 14 minutes before the field got going again. Wilson was obviously in great pain, but up to the front he went again, but the speed had very noticeably decreased.

At Leominster, there was more trouble. Road repairs made the road look like the moon's surface and there was puncture after puncture and many riders were off with chains jumping off gears.

Up the road, another 10 miles saw a level-crossing gate close in front of the race. Some got through, others chucked their bikes over the gate and clambered after them, but all managed to regroup. Wilson was still there, but Dicky Richards, his team-mate, was often to be seen giving him a friendly push when the going got a bit hard.

At Bewdley Hill, Russell and Clark (I.T.P.) shot off, and were soon being chased by six more. They caught the flying tandem, but such was the pace the I.T.P. men set that three of these were soon left out in the cold. They raced through the rain-soaked and crowded streets of Wolverhampton, and it was Ken Russell who thrashed across the line, one second in front of team-mate Geof. Clark, with Alec Taylor (Gnutti) at a wheel.

Don Wilson (Yorkshire) lost 4 minutes on the run-in and was whisked off to hospital for a check-up, and the yellow jersey remained firmly on the stocky shoulders of Dave Bedwell.

THE TOUR OF BRITAIN - 1951

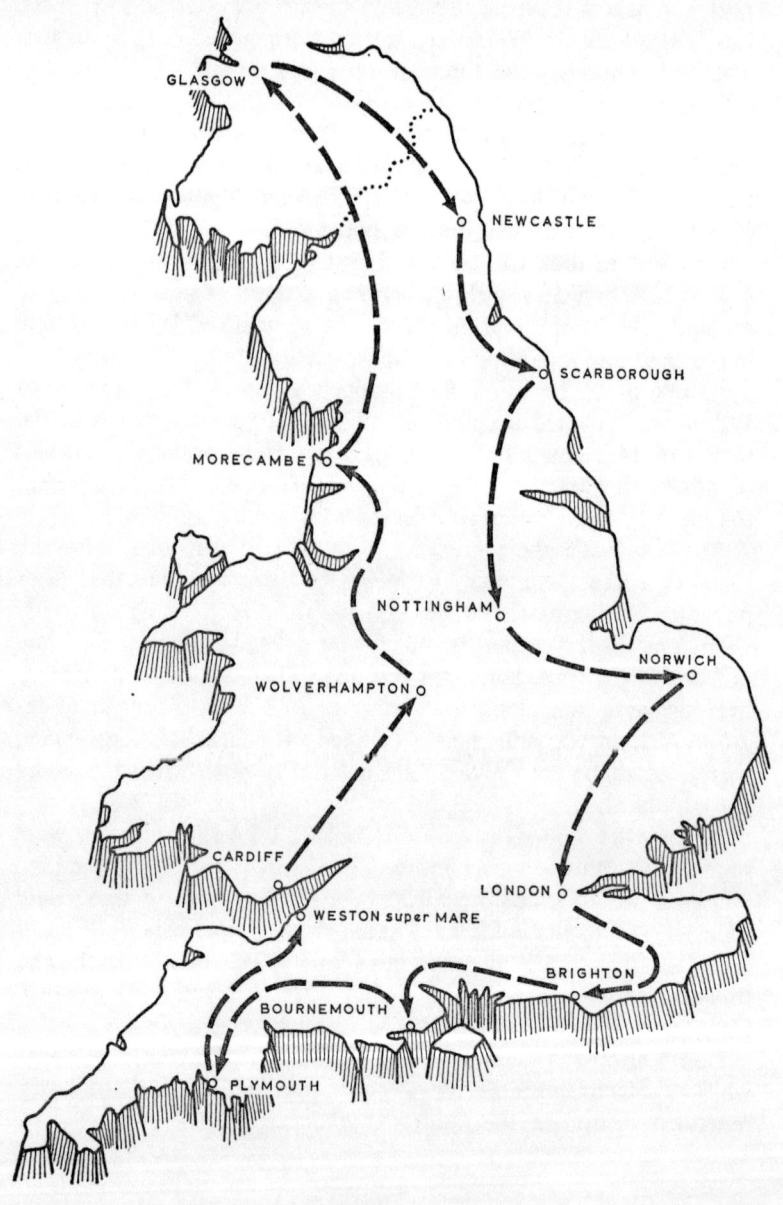

STAGE 6.   WOLVERHAMPTON TO MORECAMBE   127 MILES.

Some of the team cars were taking an even bigger 'bashing' than the riders, and there were a number with sundry bits of wire and string in evidence. Down on the start line, Don Wilson, sore, but all in one piece, was very determined that he was going on.

The day's race was long but fairly flat and they had the advantage of a following wind. A huge crowd gave them a wonderful send-off from West Park, and just outside the town things began to liven up and several sorties were made, but to no effect.

Averaging a steady 25 m.p.h. they raced on and between Ternhill and Whitchurch there was a break and before long the field was neatly split in two, with all the leading lights in the backmarkers group! At Weaverham, they were already 30 minutes up on schedule and had begun that long, horrible, night-mare run through the traffic-infested area of Warrington.

Les Scales (Dayton) breaks clear with half-a-dozen more and they soon form a fast moving echelon that sees their group getting farther and farther away. Behind them, the second group had begun to realise the real danger and Garnier (France) attacked incessantly, taking with him Ian Greenfield (Scotland), but this break died the death. Russell went and Parker (Dayton) went with him, it came to naught.

This was another unlucky day for the Irish and what with punctures, the sags, and complete inability to read a race and keep with the bunch, they were fighting a rear-guard and losing battle all the way.

Through Ashton, Wigan, Standish and Euxton they tore, crazy, crazy, and when Preston came in sight there were many in that lead bunch ready to call it a day. Scales was still out there in front hammering away, but his little bunch was disintegrating 'before his very eyes' and, as they approached Lancaster, the last of them dropped off the back, and in the second group attack after attack was being launched.

Ken Jowett nearly blew a gasket getting up to Scales, and behind him was the mad tandem of Alec Taylor (Gnutti) and Ian Steel. So hard did they hammer the pedals that, just the other side of Lancaster they caught Scales and Jowett (I.T.P.) and went by as though the pair had stopped. Another group in Russell,

27

Bedwell and Parker were chasing hard, and the bottle for team placings was really settling down. In Lancaster, Garnier 'took off' on a bend and, having somersaulted a couple of times, picked himself up, got back on his bike, and proceeded to eat ground, right through the thrashing bunch.

The tyres sang as they raced on to the Promenade, and it was Steel from Jowett pounding it out, wheel to wheel, with Taylor down by 15 seconds and Scales, grey-faced, but still trying at 40 seconds. Scotland's 6 foot Ian Steel pounded Jowett into the dust and they made the finish line with Ken at two lengths. Just 25 seconds later Alec Taylor free-wheeled in, and the plucky Les Scales made it in for fourth place, *only two seconds* in front of Parker, Bedwell, Russell and Seel (I.T.P.).

Again the *maillot jaune* goes to Bedwell, and Dayton lead in the team race.

STAGE 7. MORECAMBE TO GLASGOW 160 MILES.

This was the longest stage ever to have been ridden by any rider in Britain, and was also one of the toughest. The wind was, thankfully, behind, otherwise there might not have been a story to write. Along the sea-coast and then through Carnforth they belt and several attempts have already been made to break away.

Kendal saw Clark (I.T.P.), Buttle (Dayton) and Bloomfield (Gnutti) away, and chasing were Audemard, Steel, Blair and Nicholls (Viking) and Russell. The three stayed out there for some time, but Bloomfield 'blew' and went out through the back. On the climb up the 1,300 feet of Shap, Buttle scuttled into the lead, taking the *prime*. Down, down they sweep at 50 m.p.h. and more, and first Clark and then Buttle is reeled in and caught by the chasing group, and they have a lead of minutes. Audemard had taken a belting and had dropped back.

There are 9 in the lead now, including Greenfield, Wellman (South London) and Alec Taylor, and they formed into a fast moving snake that covered the first 50 miles in well under 2 hours! They echeloned out, taking a thrashing and after Carlisle it was Greenfield who led the charge and kept the pace high, for he dearly wanted to be the first to enter his country in triumph. As they wound it up, so his right pedal wound off, and he was left sorrowfully behind. Alec Taylor it was who took the Border *prime*, by taking lengths out of the rest of the bunch.

The mounting speed had the riders in a whirl. So tremendous was the pace that even the smallest amount of daylight was sufficient to leave a rider gasping by the wayside. Both Buttle and Russell went this way, shattered beyond relief. They hurtled over a rough patch of ground and Clark's tyre went down suddenly. Fantastically fast he changed, belting the daylights out of himself to catch the leaders, and punctured again within a mile.

Now there were but 5 left, and 3 of them Viking men, and a 100 miles went by in less than 4 hours. So far were they ahead of schedule that policemen, helpers, spectators, were amazed when the 5 swept by, over *twenty minutes* ahead of the main field.

At Lesmahagow, it was Derek Wellman the only amateur rider there, who cracked, and so it was down to 4. Three Vikings against one Gnutti, and so they proceeded to give Alec the works. Time after time they took off, one by one, only to be pulled back by Taylor, and the same thing to happen again. But it was Nicholls of Viking whose legs screamed 'enough'. He had worked hard throughout and now had to pay the penalty, but there was only a few miles to the finish.

Through Larkhall, Hamilton and Uddington they trundled, warily searching one another out, but to no avail. Down the London Road into Glasgow it was Stan Blair that led out Steel, with Taylor grimly hanging on. A bit of 'switching' goes on and Taylor suddenly finds himself unsighted on Steel, and this is the moment that Ian 'flies' and at the line it is Ian Steel, with Alec Taylor at half-a-wheel, with Blair a length away, third. Wellman scuttles in for a well-deserved fourth place, and relegates a dejected Nicholls to fifth place.

Behind them, the field is strung out from here to nowhere in particular, for many of them have taken the beating of a lifetime, and it is 22 long minutes before Bedwell comes in, suffering from an almighty cold (some said it was the draught from the leaders that caused it), and not only the *maillot jaune*, but the team race has passed from Dayton to Viking.

STAGE 8. GLASGOW TO NEWCASTLE 150 MILES.

Dave Bedwell and the Dayton riders had lost control of the race to the Viking men but were determined to get the lead back, and many were the plans made before the start of the eighth stage. It was a dull, blustery day as the 39 left in ambled out through the suburbs of Glasgow to Uddington, where the race proper started.

Even as the flag was lowered, Laurent sped away, and the field, caught tightening up their toe-straps, let him go. So Greenfield jumped and was away. Parker lets fly on the other side, and they tandemed up to the Frenchman by the time Hamilton was reached.

The wind was chilling and blustery showers added to the discomfort. Bedwell went suddenly from the back of the bunch, and by hops, skips and sprints, fanatically overhauled the three, and then the four begin to pile on the pressure, Lanark, Biggar and Broughton sped beneath their flying wheels and over the Peebles hills they romp, arriving at Peebles town with more than 2 minutes lead on the field.

Behind them, the field was at sixes and sevens. Audemard of France twice broke away, getting within half-a-minute of the leaders only to puncture. Others made only half-hearted attempts but soon got hauled back into the all-embracing fold.

After 100 miles, the flying 4 had nearly *10 minutes* on the bunch, but Ian Steel and his merry Viking men didn't seem at all concerned and still ploughed along.

Came Carter Bar, a long, draggy uphill three miles of 1 in 7 gradient. Down on the hooks the 4 got, changing down through the gears as the climb progressively got harder. Bedwell 'took off' half-way up, rising out of his saddle and suddenly going flat out. The other 3 didn't respond and so the Border *prime*, with its first bonus went to Dave, with the other 3 over 25 yards back.

Bedwell sat up, letting the other 3 come up then, once again into the rhythm that had been theirs for so many miles, and they swung swiftly down the mountainside and out of sight. Another *14 minutes* were to pass before the main bunch, including Steel, crossed the line!

Over the undulations the 4 speed, but tiredness was beginning to creep through their bones like a *malade*. At Otterburn, the lead had been cut to 10 minutes, and with 25 miles still to be covered, Steel made his move. The pace he set was phenomenal, but Audemard and Pierre of France saw the danger and got with him. They obviously couldn't catch the leaders but they were going to have a darned good try!

With 20 miles still to go, Laurent 'blew' and lost nearly 7 minutes between here and the finish. Bedwell, with the willing help of team-mate Parker who threw a 'dummy' for Greenfield, took the stage by 2½ lengths from Parker with Greenfield a further half-length, third. Three seconds under 8 minutes later, Laurent got a crafty fourth place from Bev Wood (Pennine), Steel and Len West (Dayton).

Steel still has the *maillot jaune* with Alec Taylor just over 6 minutes behind. Greenfield is at 11 minutes and Bedwell is 'coming up fast' at 14½ minutes.

STAGE 9. NEWCASTLE TO SCARBOROUGH 88 MILES.

Rain soaked clouds hung over Newcastle as they lined up for the start of the ninth. Wood and Fenwick were there, but their bikes hadn't arrived! The Pennine van had got caught up in a traffic jam (caused by the 'Tour') and when the flag was dropped for the 'off', the unhappy pair had to borrow a couple of machines from a service vehicle and start on those. The Pennine van shot ahead and just outside Gateshead a swop was made and the luckless two thankfully whipped on to the back of the bunch on their own machines.

Up at the front, Ian Steel had seen daylight and had let loose, and had soon opened up a big lead. It was unfortunate for him that Derek Buttle had gone with him, for he was Steel's 'watch-dog' for the day and just sat on Ian's back wheel and let him do all the work. Despite threats, cajoling and pleas, Buttle refused to work (which was his right!) and after thirty hard and dirty miles, Steel was like a wet rag and they were caught.

Bedwell immediately attacked, shooting out of the back of the bunch like a rocket, and Buttle went too. Up fast came two Irishmen, McCarthy and Lennon, and then Mick Howarth (Northern) and Nicholls. As they got down to the essentials, the heavens opened and the blistering drizzle turned into a real, right homely downpour.

31

They scudded, like oarsmen, through Ormesby and Guisborough, the chilling rain not slowing them one bit. Cox of the boat was Bedwell, keeping them in line and pedalling at the right pace. Up Buck Brow they plodded, with Lennon going out the back like a bolt from a bow, and Dave takes the *prime* with ease. It was nearly 3 minutes before Steel's marauding party reached the Brow, only to find the fugitives well and truly gone.

Over the moors round Ruswarp the rain stopped and a mist took its place that chills the riders to the bone. Bedwell now takes on the role of 'shop steward' and the five sped along, working like beavers in their endeavour to get further and further away from the chasers, and it is Bedwell, the Trojan worker, who scurried hither and yon, making sure that the pressure was being put on in the right place and where it hurt most.

Those behind were endeavouring to give chase, but Bedwell's team-mates were putting a stop to every move, and the grim battle is fought out, yard by struggling yard. At Sneaton, the runaways have a lead of 5 minutes, and the sccchwish of the tyres made a merry song as they hurtle towards Scarborough.

Buttle, under instruction, led out, with McCarthy, Howarth and Nicholls fighting for his wheel. Bedwell took a mighty leap round their side and rocketed across the line a length in front of Buttle, with McCarthy, at a wheel, third.

It was 5 minutes and 16 seconds later that Ian Steel crossed the line, still, it is true, race leader, and Taylor was still second, but Bedwell . . . mighty Dave was now only 7 minutes 52 seconds behind Steel, and that was certainly something for Ian to think about on the second 'rest day'.

We record with regret that it was on this stage that the cigar-smoking 'Duke' (Jimmy Saville) gave up the race ghost, and became the cigar-smoking, non-stop talking race announcer that has gradually given way to one of the greatest disc-jockeys of all time!

STAGE 10. SCARBOROUGH TO NOTTINGHAM 125 MILES.

The fantastic rise of Bedwell over his misfortunes will always be a talking point of ifs and buts, for it was truly spectacular riding that had pulled this tiny dynamo back from 22 minutes

The incident at Newhaven during the 1951 Tour of Britain when an official carried Audemards' bike over the bridge and cost him a 30 seconds penalty

The field hammering through Newmarket on Stage 12, Tour of Britain 1951

Eugene Garnier of France waves as he comes in first during the final stage of the 1951 Tour of Britain

Jimmy Saville, disc-jockey extraordinary, who rode in the first Tour of Britain and lasted until the end of the ninth stage, after which he took up announcing on the Tour

down to only 8 with only 3 stages to go. Little did we know that this stage was to be even more spectacular than the previous 2, as they stood in the pouring rain, waiting for the Mayor of Scarborough to give them the 'off'.

Out of sea-girt Scarborough they trundled, the cold wetness not dampening their spirits, although many of them, through so much rain on the 'Tour' were down to the bare essentials in clothing. Geof. Clark (I.T.P.) soon had to call it a day, an old knee injury being the cause.

Eastwood (Northern) and Ken Jowett slipped the leash after 20 miles, and by Malton had been joined by Bev. Wood, Len West, the two Wilsons and Frank Seel. The rain sloshed down as they formed a group that worked well together and soon they had a very nice lead.

The 7 belted through Norton, bearing right, and were immediately out of sight. A policeman stepped out, looked up the road waiting for the rest of the riders, and managed to cover up the rain-soaked arrows.

Disaster struck the field for, instead of bearing right, they went to the left, and no-one bothered to stop them and, in a very short while were well and truly 'up-the-spout'. A couple of minutes later, the organiser, Doug Peakall came booming over a narrow humped-back bridge in his 'Jag' and met another official, in another 'Jag' coming the other way. Result . . . two dented 'Jaguars'!

Meanwhile, Bedwell, Scales, Parker and Phillips (the first three of the Dayton team) had dropped back in Malton for Derek Buttle who was feeling ill, and they too had gone 'off course'.

The leading 7 happily hammered on, unaware of the confusion behind. The field, by now well on the wrong course, first threatened to strike, then when they found this didn't work, became *malade* and got slower and slower, with the Bedwell party, well lost and struggling to find the rest of the bunch. *Never at any time was this group any more than 1 minute and 10 seconds behind the main bunch,* and this has a sequel at the end of the stage. Both the main bunch, and the Bedwell group were to do many more miles than they should have done.

And so, they came out on the right road at last, and a very helpful police superintendent gathered them together along York's wall, until they were all safely gathered in, that is, minus the

Bedwell bunch. They changed clothes, ate, tinkered with bikes, and were then sent on their way, when the luckless ones finally came up.

Down through Snaith, Thorne and Bawtry the seven amble, for they have been told of what has happened and the field is something like 50 minutes behind them now. At Ollerton there were five, for Eastwood and Jim Wilson (Yorkshire) had departed and were to finish back with the bunch. On the other side of Ollerton, Don Wilson also called it a day, and lost a heck of a lot of time between here and the Nottingham finish.

Through the traffic-infested run-in they sped, all four jockeying for position and it was Len West (Dayton) who slithered by Jowett and Bev. Wood (Pennine) to take the stage. Don Wilson glided in 5 minutes later, and that was *exactly* the time given to the next 28 riders, which included Steel, Taylor and Greenfield. Behind them, the Bedwell group was given a 'token' time of 3 minutes and 10 seconds more.

It was obvious that, apart from the first 4, the rest of the race times should have been nullified, but no matter how much argument the Dayton team, who were the main losers, put up, nothing could alter the official decision. From here on it was all argy-bargy, and the wrangling went on well into the night.

There are too many 'perhaps' for a logical conclusion to be reached, but without doubt, the stage had wrought untold disaster on a very fine race.

STAGE 11. NOTTINGHAM TO NORWICH 123 MILES.

The Dayton team lined up, still seething with disgust at the treatment meted out to them the night before, and their hearts weren't really in it. The sun shone, tis true, but heavy black clouds in the distance had already begun to gather.

Such was the lack of enthusiasm among the riders, etc., that the first 15 miles took 43 minutes, and it wasn't until near Botteford that an attack came, and then from a real surprise quarter.

It was Scotland's young Addie who belted into the lead, to be followed by McCarthy of Ireland and Laurent of France. The League of Nations got away and they changed rapidly, allowing no daylight and soon the hard work began to pay dividends. At

Grantham they had built up a lead of 3 minutes, and as they shot through the town, the course swung suddenly and they ran into a nasty side-wind.

It didn't seem to bother them as they started the long climb up to Spittlegate where Laurent took the *prime* and the course swung again . . . into a headwind. As the wind screamed round them the pace dropped to a mere 20 m.p.h. but their rhythmic riding was keeping them away and, at Fosdyke, 52 miles from the start, and as they passed through the feeding station they had a lead of 9 minutes on the bunch, and 6 minutes on a very lonely Eastwood.

After the feeding station, Steel got browned off and shot away, but Alec Taylor and Pierre of France also got the urge and within a mile had become a chasing trio. How they worked! Rhythmic poetry in motion, with a change and change about, echeloning to the right and then the left as direction changed, never staying at the front longer than necessary and, all the time pulling back the leading three puppets, and gathering Eastwood as they hurtled along. With only 20 miles to go they had pulled back the leading 3 to only 4 minutes.

What a chase it was from here! Eastwood had 'died the death' and the flying three left him crawling along at a snail's pace. Times were bandied back and forth, and the lead gradually dwindled as the miles dropped still more slowly. Dave Addie had had his day, and with death in his legs, let McCarthy and Laurent go.

On long, straight stretches of road, the chasing three had Addie in their sights and this spurred them on to greater efforts to gather him in and race on to catch the others. It was not to be however, for Andre Laurent crossed the finishing line a length ahead of Karl McCarthy, just 45 seconds in front of the hurtling 4.

The lackadaisical bunch ambled in anything from 2 minutes 23 seconds to nearly an hour and a quarter later, and all was certainly not right in the camp! The arguing over the time adjustment on the 10th stage still went on and was fast getting out of hand, and this led up to a situation that never ought to have been allowed.

STAGE 12. NORWICH TO LONDON 115 MILES.

This is it! The dream of every bike rider. The last and final stage and the hopes of finishing high in the General Classification. There was a strong wind blowing as Ian Steel donned the last stage *maillot jaune* and, after the preliminaries, the flag was waved, and the riders were under way for the last time.

And just as suddenly, the whole Dayton team stopped, got off their bikes and, under instruction from their sponsors, withdrew from the race. What a real tragedy this was! Around them, there were murmurs of sympathy from the crowds, and from many of the riders, for the whole team had fought long, valiantly, and well.

This left but 33 to contest the stage and at Hethersett, after 5½ miles had gone by, they were still all together. At 10 miles, Dave Addie took a flyer and disappeared 'up the road'. It lasted for 4 long, hard, lonely and senseless miles, and then he was back in the fold.

As they caught Addie, Garnier of France went, and Joe Lennon of Ireland went with him. Addie again leapt to life, nearly taking Joe's wheel from under him, and off the three galloped, making what hay they could while the rain came down.

The drag through Thetford, Mildenhall and Newmarket saw them working hard and long and, by the time 60 miles had gone by they had a nice lead of 5 minutes. The loopy-loop of Six Mile Bottom was where the 'feed' took place, and they picked up their musettes with care before speeding on their way.

Down to Royston, and the lead was 10 minutes, and at Baldock, it had increased to 13 minutes. There was no move in the bunch, for none of these 3 had anything except a stage win to gain, but the pace was raised and after Stevenage, the rumble had become a roar, and the lead had pulled back to 8 minutes.

At Welwyn, Ian Steel put out feelers and got pulled back, but his flying legs revved faster and faster and finally he drew away, and at Mill Hill was only five minutes behind the hammering three.

Through the streets of London on the way to Hampstead, Lennon came a purler on the wet roads, skidding along some yards, and opening up old wounds. Gamely he got up, blood dripping everywhere, got on his bike, and putting everything into that last bit got back with the other two. Into West Heath Road they pounded, taking time out to jockey for position, and it was Eugene Garnier who worked out all the possible angles to take the stage, with Joe Lennon of Ireland a length away, with Dave Addie of Scotland getting his so richly deserved third place.

They were bandaging Lennon up as Steel belted in to take 4th place, 4 minutes and 36 seconds later, covered from head to foot in mud from a crash only 4 miles from the finish, and he was on team-mate Fred Nicholls bike. Behind him the bunch were at 14 seconds and the first 'Tour of Britain' was over with Ian Steel, Viking 1st; Alec Taylor, Gnutti 2nd at 6 minutes 16 seconds and Ian Greenfield, Scotland, 3rd another 5 minutes and 50 seconds back. The Team race went to Viking too, for they beat the French team by over 40 minutes and despite the fact that the Dayton team had voluntarily retired, the 'King of the Mountains' prize went to one, Dave Bedwell, the strong man of the 'Tour'.

3: The 'Loner's' Tour

Tour of Britain, 1952
August 22nd—September 6th

Ye olde castle dominated sea-side town of Hastings had probably never seen the like of it before, and probably never will again. There were literally thousands out to see this colourful cavalcade of sport called the 'Tour of Britain' and, despite the 'kill-joys' within the Union's ranks, they were thoroughly enjoying the spectacle.

78 riders were there, waiting to start, and around them was the hub-bub of sound associated with great sporting occasions. The pattern was the same this year – Independent (near professional) riders in sponsored teams, together with a number of 'amateur' teams, and with six International teams from France, Belgium, Italy, West Germany, Ireland and Scotland. The French, Irish and West Germans were from dissident bodies, while the Italians and Belgians were 'unregistered', which made the whole a real 'rebel' body.

The 'rebel' League was beginning to grow from strength to strength, and had taken the cream of the Union's 'massed-start' men, and they rode in this event under the sponsorship of B.S.A. Cycles.

Interest had been worked up over the weeks before, not only through Ian Steel's great win in the first 'Tour of Britain', but in the fact that, in early May of 1952 he, and a good all-round team of riders had gone out, under the managership of Percy Stallard and the auspices of the League, to compete in and explore the possibilities of the 14-day Warsaw-Berlin-Prague (which had aptly been named the 'Peace Race'). Not only had Steel won this international race convincingly, and in the face of tremendously power-

38

ful opposition from 13 other countries, but the team had won the team award as well!

The *Express* had, of course, cashed in on the resultant publicity, and through this, virtually overnight, cycling . . . always a 'Cinderella' sport had become popular throughout the length and breadth of the country.

So there they all were, performing the 'last rites'; the massaging of legs; the adjustment of gears; putting food into jersey pockets; doing the little odd jobs that keep the mind off the race to come. Some were old hands and knew the ropes, just sitting back relaxed and enjoying the whole. Others were 'first-timers', and neither knew whether to laugh or cry; shout or sing; sit or stand up, so auspicious was the occasion to them.

Carlisle Parade was blocked off for the assembly and beneath the summer's day clear blue sky, the Mayor made his speech of welcome and is introduced to some of the riders. As they walked down the line, it was explained to him that they have nearly 1,500 miles to ride and that each day's stage was a race in itself, with each day's time being accumulated against each rider, with the winner of the race being the one who, at the finish, had the lowest time.

The preliminaries are brought to a close, and the Mayor and his entourage proceeded leisurely to the Start line. Motorbike marshals revved-up machines and the lead car moved slowly off, followed by the marshals. All was set for the great moment, and slowly the timekeeper read out the seconds to go.

All around, silence had descended on the vast crowds – the flag was raised – riders gripped 'bars tighter, one foot already in the strap. 5, 4, 3, 2, 1, Go . . . down came the flag and the colourful 78 set off on their 16 day journey round Britain.

STAGE 1. HASTINGS TO SOUTHSEA 99 MILES.

Through the cheering crowds the cavalcade ride and out through Silverhill to the Battle Road, aptly named perhaps, for this was where battle commenced. Legs began to revolve faster, gears were snapped into smaller sprockets and already tentative moves were made to feel out opponents, but they made no impression. The undulations to Battle are taken in their stride and the race settled into a leisurely pace with the whole field in one bunch.

Nobody wanted to be at the front on his own but, as the speed mounted up into the 30's man after man shot off the front, stayed 'out in space' for a few seconds of time and then was gathered into the maelstrom of the bunch.

Along the switchback road they tore, with tactics being used by the foreigners that had scarcely been seen in this country before. They weaved across the road from side to side; cut corners by the barest fraction, forcing those behind to swing wide; took advantage of parked cars to nearly take the wheel of the man behind from under him. In fact, they did everything that was legal, but in a different way.

Quite suddenly, everything slowed, and the field sat up to get its breath back. Not so Johnny Brackstone, the 21 year old tool-maker from London, for he saw his chance and took it. Out of the saddle, a gigantic sprint, and he was away and, after 14 miles, the first break of the 'Tour' was on. Behind him, others too had seen the opportunity and had let fly and a group of 8 were pounding the pedals, determined to get up with this young upstart.

They did and, working like maniacs, proceeded to get as much daylight and time as they could between themselves and the chasing bunch. Mile after mile the torture went on, echelons working up and down to a hairsbreadth, maintaining a fast and truly killing speed, which eventually blew Tony Smith of Romford straight out of the back.

Twenty-five miles were covered in the first hour, and between the main bunch and the leaders were four smaller groups. Down to Patcham, and up its hill, the leaders got strung out, and it was Bob Maitland (B.S.A.) who took the first *prime*, leading over Yeaman (Pennine) and Brackstone (London). Only 4 more followed them, so one more had disappeared 'into the blue'.

It was a good 2 minutes before the next group appeared and these 8 were led by Pierre of France. It was obvious that they had been working really hard, and sweat mingled with the greyness of their faces. Another 2 minutes went by before the main bunch appeared.

Just after Patcham, at the feeding station, Ian Steel hit dirt. A rider skidded in front of him after hitting a dropped feeding bottle, and Ian belted into him and fell on to the grass verge. No damage to him, only his bike, which he continued to use through to the finish.

Each rise now saw the leaders trying to maintain their dignity, while the chasers got nearer and nearer. Close to Offington, Les Drinkwater's legs cried for mercy and there was a septet chasing a septet. As they climbed out of Arundel they joined up, greetings were exchanged, some not too politely, and then down to the business of putting even more than the 2½ minutes which separated them from the main bunch.

No tentative moves were made for there was the finish to contest. Along Chichester's By-pass they screamed, each man taking his turn at the front, even if only for a few seconds. Havant saw them in a flurry of wheels and soon they appeared at the end of Southsea's Serpentine Road.

The whole 14 got down to it in the same second, and 14 different coloured jerseys hurled themselves and their machines towards the line in a fantastic blaze of colour. It was every man for himself and, in line abreast they came forward with Johnny Brackstone getting the verdict by a gnat's whisker, from Ken Russell (Ellis-Briggs), and Ken Jowett (R.A.F.) third, with all the rest of the package deal in the same time. With 3 men in this group, the B.S.A. team lead in the team race.

STAGE 2. SOUTHSEA TO WEYMOUTH 85½ MILES.

The sun shone in all its glory, and all was right with the World as the field lined up for the second stage. The Lord Mayor of Portsmouth helped Brackstone don the *maillot jaune*, the race leader's jersey, amidst thunderous applause, not only from the sporting crowd, but from the riders as well.

Dogged by dozens of club cyclists they trundled out of Southsea, like some gigantic club run, to the start proper, 5¼ miles away on the A.27. Once they were let loose, nothing stayed with them for the speed was tremendous. Attack followed attack, but those that did get away wished they hadn't and came back as though on elastic.

For 33, long, hard and fast miles they remained as one and, as the climb of Stoney Cross approached, toe-straps were tightened, eyes roamed round for the slightest movement of a break, and

Maitland and Welch (Viking) just went. Behind them, Len West (Sun), Proctor, Audemard, Don Wilson and 'Tiny' Thomas saw the move, and there was daylight where they once were.

With 7 men spread across the road, there was little room for anything else and it was crazy, crazy climbing all the way. Welch and Maitland were swallowed as though by a tidal wave, and it was Proctor (B.S.A.) who took the *prime* from West and Aldridge (Romford). Then they all sat up and let the panting bunch catch them! Behind them 2 West Germans and 2 Italians had found the going too hard, and Thomas, Newman and Jones of B.S.A. were trying to make it back after 'Tiny' had punctured.

Up at the front, nine men 'go-man-go' and were slowly but surely putting daylight where once was none. Within 9 miles, 8 more got the idea and belted off the front, including Lackey of Ireland and 3 Belgians. At Wareham, the leaders had just under 2½ minutes on this group, with the main bunch at a further minute.

There were 7 miles to go at Warmwell Cross, and the leaders were told that they had now only a 1 minute lead, and it was panic stations. They hustled themselves into formation and charged on towards the finish. Through Preston they sped, jockeying for position and along the sea-wall into Weymouth. Don Wilson (Yorkshire) was there, as was Johnny Welch, Gregorini of France, Norman Yeaman (Pennine) and Ken Russell.

As they pounded in towards the finish at Greenhill Gardens, it was Russell who burst from the back, taking the pole line and leaving no doubt by a 3 length win over Gregorini and Don Wilson that he was the master on that day. The rest of the merry 9 were all placed, Stan Blair (Viking) coming last, 2 seconds behind Russell.

The rest started to come in, 1 minute and 19 seconds after, with Brackstone at 3 minutes and 5 seconds, which gave the yellow jersey to Russell. Fernand Maestri of Italy was the first to retire.

STAGE 3. WEYMOUTH TO WESTON SUPER MARE 74 MILES.

So Ken Russell, the 'loner', with no team to back him up donned the *maillot jaune* and 77 men pedalled sedately out of

Weymouth, hell-bent on getting to their destination as quickly as possible. For mile after mile the relentless pace was kept up, with no give or take. No one, but no one gets, and the crowds in the towns and villages passed through had the sight of one huge mass of riders passing before them, all in one group.

As they climbed up from Dorchester, Van den Dooren (Belgium) whipped away smartly and got a 3 length lead of Ken Jowett and Charlie Mather (Manchester) to take the *prime*, but they immediately came back to the bunch.

This gigantic group moved forward maintaining its equilibrium all the while, the maelstrom erupting from the centre, out to the edges and back in again. After 40 miles and outside Compton, there was a sudden gap and 32 riders detached themselves. Far away to the rear Ziegler of Germany was struggling with a high temperature and looked decidedly green.

As the 2 groups pounded through Wells, Cheddar, Axbridge and Banwell, there was little or no movement in their ranks. The 32 kept moving up a few seconds every mile, while one or two laggards got lost from the back of the second group.

It wasn't until the final few miles that the big bunch began to spread their wings, and then, from first to last man was but a few seconds. Speed became their god as they hurtled down from Uphill and into Weston Super Mare. They hit Beach Road *en masse* and no finessing was necessary for there was no room to do so.

In line, and fantastically fast they sprinted towards the line. Palings bulged as spectators leant forward to get a better look. The bulgings caused those on the outside to push more into the centre, and then . . . it was all happening!

There was a rending of metal, the bang of tyres bursting and, amidst the spectators and following vehicles lay 6 riders. Those behind were forced to stop, or ride over, or round the tangled mass of bleeding bodies and damaged machines.

The lucky ones who got through kept going and on the line it was Stan Jones (B.S.A.) from Sanchez of Italy, with 'Tiny' Thomas third. They came in, these couriers in ones and twos, some dragging, some carrying their machines, but all determined to finish. Some collapsed after finishing, and Proctor, Drinkwater, Kopitz (Germany) and Jowett were taken to hospital. At the roadside, Wightman (Sun) had treatment, while others were treated for shock.

It was obvious that the Judges had not kept their eyes on the riders but on the crash, and after due deliberation, all 32 riders were credited equal 6th in the same time as the winner.

The decks were just about clear when the second group appeared and crossed the line. B.S.A. still led the team race and Ken Russell the *maillot jaune*.

After being patched up, the riders crossed by ferry boat to Cardiff to spend the night, while officials did a Monte Carlo Rally round the peninsular, through Gloucester and so to Cardiff, arriving well after midnight.

STAGE 4.   CARDIFF TO ABERYSTWYTH $109\frac{1}{2}$ MILES.

They gathered in brilliant sunshine in the forecourt of the Civic Centre of Cardiff for the 'off'. 3 were not there. Kopitz and Jowett who were too bruised from the previous day's crash, and the German, Ziegler, still detained in hospital.

There were a few rumblings from the foreign riders because of lack of food, which wasn't surprising, because rationing was still in force. Steaks, even of horse-meat were hard to come by, and in the countries of the main complainants, France and Italy, were virtually non-existent.

But all 73 got off to a processional start and just outside Cardiff the leash was sprung and the race was on over the rough and tumble of roads through the Central Welsh mountains. They kept together, but not by intent, more by instinct, for within 7 miles of the start they had to climb Caerphilly Mountain and it was here that Wightman, suffering greatly from his previous day's injuries, got shot off. Here too, went Morrish of Ireland with gear trouble, and eventually he joined forces with Wightman.

The descent was dicey, and De Smit, Thomson and Pierre took a hair-pin bend a bit too fast, ran out of road, and came an almighty cropper. Thomson (Scotland) was in a half-daze but remounted and pressed on, and De Smit (Belgium) and Pierre went along too.

It was a gradual climb for 28 miles to the top of the Brecon Beacons, 2,000 feet above sea-level, and the field split and then split again. Out of Merthyr Tydfil 9 men led, 6 of them amateurs. They were being chased by a group of 6, and then a 3 man group, with behind them, the main bunch at 3 minutes. Stan Jones took the *prime* and, on the descent, although the 9 stayed away, behind them a chasing group of 13 formed up.

From Sennybridge to Llandovery the chase was on in earnest and many a private battle was fought out on this stretch but, on the hill from Llandovery, the leaders were well and truly caught, and the group was now 22 strong. Johnny Pound (Yorkshire) took a horrible pounding, and that was his day. Greenfield kept his balance on a softening tyre, which just had to be changed at the feeding station, and that left twenty.

15 miles from Aberystwyth, as the crow flies, stands Trichrug, only 1,007 feet above sea level but, from the Talsarn side it rises from 200 feet to 1,000 feet in less than two miles. After the long, dragging climbs of the previous hills this was a 'freak' climb and Charles Gregorini seized this moment to go through the field like a scythe. What a tremendous performance this was as rider after rider was left struggling, panting and derelict in the rear. Within a mile he had gained a lead of over 1 minute and, not waiting to see what had happened to the rest tore on.

Down, down he sprinted, out of the saddle and moving fantastically fast and soon was out of sight. Scales, Russell, Thomas, Steel and even Greenfield settled down to the chase, but were not to see him again before the finish.

Gregorini of France went up and over Glanrhos as though the Devil himself was behind him and burst into Aberystwyth at amazing speed, even sprinting, out of the saddle, the length of the South Marine Terrace. And what a tremendous welcome he got! From this really great performance he was to climb from 27th to 4th place on General Classification.

In 10 seconds over 2 minutes, 14 more riders contested the sprint for the line, and Les Scales took second place, only inches in front of yellow-shirted, Ken Russell, who now held the lead by nearly 3 minutes.

The rumblings over grub became a torrent. Food in this town was not easy to come by, outside of rations, for you must remember that this was a seaside town, 'out in the sticks' and trying desperately hard to get over the war years. The organisers and officials did everything they could to get more food, but didn't, it seems, get enough.

STAGE 5. ABERYSTWYTH TO BLACKPOOL 179 MILES.

This was to be, and is to this day, the longest stage of any 'Tour of Britain', and it went right across Wales, up into the 'black country' with a swing back to the coast at Blackpool. As the riders lined up it was announced that the entire French and Italian teams had withdrawn from the race.

Along the seafront they meandered and out on the road to Machynlleth. Before they reached the town 8 men had got clear and had a lead of 1½ minutes and, on the wind-swept climb up Mynydd Gwern, O'Reilly (Ireland) lost contact, and it seemed as though he'd had it. Not so! Within half a mile he had recovered and went through the other 7 like a sharp knife, taking the *prime* by a good 100 yards, but getting caught on the descent. They had a lead of 2 minutes.

7 more began to chase and, up to Bala they had caught the leaders, and it was these 15 who had a lead of 4 minutes on the next bunch. Apart from O'Reilly and Hawkins (Ireland) all were to stay together until the finish. Rain was threatening as Fenwick took the £10 Border *prime* at Queensferry.

In the lead bunch were Steel, Pottier and Blair (Viking), Bodson and Van den Dooren (Belgium), Ken Russell, Les Scales and a number of amateurs, and the only B.S.A. rider there was Pete Proctor. 'Tiny' Thomas was having an off day, collecting puncture after puncture which dropped him from 2nd place down to 18th place before the day was out.

Through Warrington and Wigan, with a 5 minute lead (it must have been taken with a sun-dial!) the 15 hurried with no holds barred, and close to Wigan Pier the Irish lads said 'goodbye'. Steel tried a few feelers but Russell soon had him in tow and after Euxton, Ian gave up the struggle. Through Preston, Ian tried once more, scorching round a bend and gaining yards to try and get away, but Ken latched on, and so it was 13 of the best that turned towards Blackpool for the run-in. Some official observers gave their lead as 3 minutes.

There was, of course, no photo-finish camera available and everything was by 'vision', and to this day I think the officials made an error because, although they gave *all 13* the same time, while perhaps a poor judge *might* have placed all the first 4 on the same second, the next 2 were *at least* 3 seconds back, 2 more at 5 seconds back, 2 at 6 seconds back, and the last 2 at 8 and 10 seconds back.

This is borne out by photographs of the finish and, although these were taken a yard *before* the line, they were taken as authentic and although the judges (rightly in my opinion) gave the verdict to Les Scales, after seeing the photograph, this decision was reversed and the verdict given to Ken Russell.

It was less than *1 minute* after their arrival, that the 200-yard flag went up again, and 8 more warriors, including 2 more B.S.A. men rode in. They had pulled back 2 minutes in less than 20 miles, or were the sun-dials working overtime? Russell's lead, by his very lucky win was now 4 minutes, and Viking's chances of taking over the team race were negligible.

With the finish the storm came and rain lashed down during the 'rest day' in the cowboy-hatted seaside town.

STAGE 6. BLACKPOOL TO CARLISLE   90 MILES.

The gale force winds had dropped but the sky was still overcast with black hanging clouds as the order came for the start. Russell had donned his yellow jersey to a standing ovation and the Tower was left behind as they pedalled out on to the Garstang road. Another 5 miles went by before they were let loose.

Everyone wanted to put the bite on, but such was the speed that at Lancaster they were already 8 minutes up on schedule and all together, and going like an express train. On the 'flats' towards Kendal, 6 broke loose and headed north and before long, 8 more, including Les Scales crept away and joined them, and through Kendal and up to Shap they galloped.

It's not steep, this climb, more of a grind than anything else, and it took some time to get down through the cogs, some, 'tis true, longer than others, and the lead bunch stretched out like so much elastic. Len West (Sun) made all the running, taking the *prime* by 150 yards from Ian Greenfield.

5 went through Clinton, followed closely by 5 more, and it was here that Len West punctured. Behind them, Russell was having a do-or-die effort with Steel and Stan Jones, for Ian had come up from behind and was all set to climb the General Class ladder. One by one they tried every known tactic, and a few that hadn't been tried before, which virtually led to the point of exhaustion. They finally gave up the struggle and were caught by a bunch of 12 riders.

The lead group now contained Bill Bellamy (Romford) who was but 4 minutes behind Russell, and he cajoled and pushed this bunch to the length of its tether, keeping the pace moving, setting the trend, never letting go, just like a terrier with a bone, and as Carlisle came in sight, the lead had stretched to more than 4 minutes.

There were 9 to contest the sprint in the London Road, and the 87 official miles had stretched to 90. Placed second on stages 4 and 5, Les Scales made this one his very own, winning by a length from Johnny Pottier (Viking) and with Bev. Wood (Pennine) in third spot, at inches.

They stood around anxiously after the finish, for the grape-vine had given all sorts of times that the main bunch was behind them, but it was a little over $4\frac{1}{4}$ minutes later that 16 riders swept across the line.

Bill Bellamy, an amateur, had taken the lead by a mere 11 seconds from Ken Russell, and hadn't once, in all the 6 stages, been in the first three!

STAGE 7. CARLISLE TO GLASGOW 96 MILES.

Rain threatened as Bellamy, in his bright new *maillot jaune* led out the remaining 59 riders, on this, the half-way day of fourteen days of racing. Just on the outskirts of Carlisle the flag was dropped and away they went, helter-skelter for the Scottish border and the 'special' prize.

As one man they rose from their saddle and sprinted like mad, and then came a nine-mile furore of movement without parallel. Shoulder to shoulder, wheel to wheel, never giving or receiving an inch they hurtled towards Gretna at over 30 m.p.h. There was but 50 yards to go to the bridge when there was a slight let-up and

Tony Phillips (Romford) raced ahead and took the *prime* from club-mate Tony Smith.

After 25 miles they were still in there punching and it was after Lockerbie that 11 managed to detach themselves and formed into a fast, hell-bent breakaway. All 11 contested the gruelling climb of Beattock and at the top of the steep and twisting hill it was 'Tiny' Thomas who just managed to get over the line first.

The 11 battle on, but 10 more were chasing like mad and by Crawford, 53 miles, they had latched on and made up a bunch nearly as large as the one to their rear. They made road, slipping through the echelons so prettily, like ballerinas at their bars. The 21 felt as though they couldn't be caught, but they reckoned without the might of Steel.

He slipped the collar of the main bunch and set out for his home town, and with him went six more. Mile after relentless mile he stayed at the front, towing them slowly, but very surely up to the front bunch. 2 laggards from the leaders were passed and got lost in the slipstream that was Steel. He forced the pace up and up, with the 6 now waggling like a tail at the rear.

At Hamilton he had them in his sights, and by Townhead Street he had caught them. There were now 26 men to contest the sprint and, although all were given the same time, all should have been placed down to 14th position. Van den Dooren got the verdict by the lick of a postage stamp, with Bev. Wood at inches, and 'Tiny' getting 3rd place.

Bellamy retained his lead of 11 seconds on Russell, and the R.A.F. team, through the loss of Thomson, who had stomach trouble, were now down to 3 men.

STAGE 8. GLASGOW TO DUNDEE 85 MILES.

Only 55 left in now and Brackstone, first day stage winner had been advised not to start, as he had a very heavy cold, but there he was, ready, willing, but not quite able. To add to his misery, the time schedule for the day had been tightened for it was a fairly easy stage to Dundee.

Off they went, and already it's over the 30 m.p.h. mark. A couple skidded on the tram-lines and Van den Dooren (Belgium) and Ron Johnson of London contemplated their wet saddles as they wearily climbed back on. Van den Dooren had a gash on his

THE TOUR OF BRITAIN - 1952

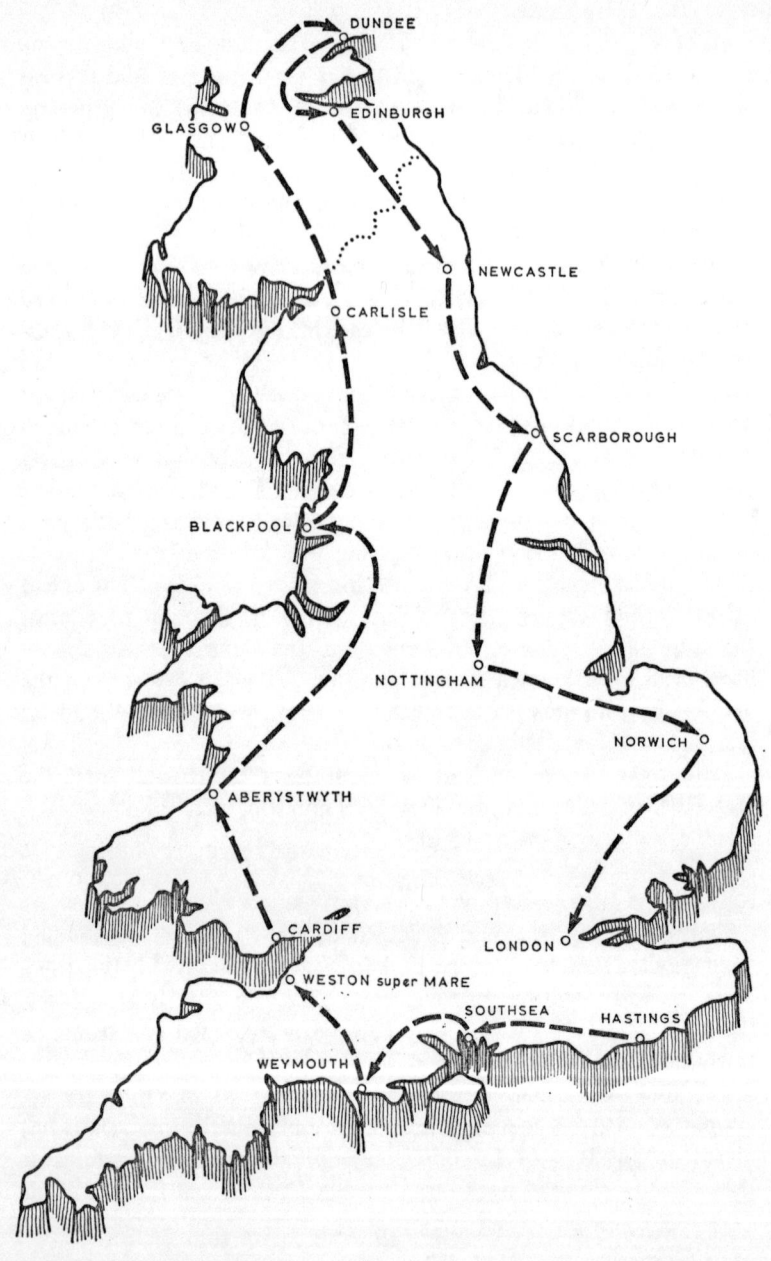

back, while Johnson had little drips of blood all over the place, but they pedalled mightily and caught the tail-end of the field just outside Glasgow.

They threw everything, race wise into it but it took 43 miles of hectic, strenuous racing before anyone could make a break and then four, in Greenfield, Stan Jones, Christison, (R.A.F.) and Hawkins (Ireland) just forced a lead. The danger was seen immediately and they were pulled back. Poor Johnny Brackstone, grey-faced and hardly able to speak and cramping up rapidly, dropped off the back, but just would not give up.

Over halfway, at Aberuthven, Greenfield got the bit between his teeth and took the day's *prime* from Proctor and Maitland. They eased off suddenly, but so did the bunch. 'Tiny' Thomas took an almighty chance and the gamble paid off. Before the field had a chance to recover, he had a lead of a hundred yards, and nine in Maitland, Scales, Newman, Greenfield, Robinson, Newman (B.S.A.), Meade and Marr (Scotland) and Fraser (R.A.F.) were haring off after him and, within 2 miles formed up and made a group of 10 that rode like men possessed.

Ken Russell knew that he had to get there, and shot out of the bunch like a bolt from the blue, and Mather (Manchester) got in his slip-stream and went with him. It took them 15 long and punishing miles to make contact, passing Meade who had unshipped his chain just as they did so. This left 11 likely lads to pound through Invergowrie, and here Les Scales felt his front tyre softening.

There were just 4 miles to go, and Les must have prayed mightily hard, and he gave no sign to the others of his dilemma. Up towards the finishing line they pounded and Robinson stopped suddenly as his gear wrapped itself lovingly round his back wheel.

Ian Steel wanted this one badly, but let fly too soon. As he slowed, so 4 more in Thomas, Russell, Maitland and Scales inched round him. Scales, with his near flat front tyre was out there in front, with every bump hammering the last bit of air out of the tyre and he held the bike upright, and made straight for the line, getting the verdict from 'Tiny' by half-a-wheel, with Ken Russell 3rd, at another half-wheel.

And so, the 'loner', Ken Russell, without team-mates, was once again overall leader and took the coveted *maillot jaune*.

STAGE 9.   DUNDEE TO EDINBURGH   91½ MILES.

The strong wind, which had helped them on the previous stage, now blew in their faces as they headed back towards Perth. Brackstone, with a high temperature and in bed with the 'flu was a nonstarter. Even with the wind dead in their faces less than 10 miles went by before Howarth, Wood and Michaux (Belgium) forced a break. By 15 miles, 6 more had got up there, and then there were 9.

Ian Steel it was, who took them up there. He jumped mightily from the back of the bunch and Proctor and Newman (B.S.A.) went with him, taking Manchester men, Mather and Clarke, with them. Don Wilson (Yorkshire) having a whale of a time and not to be outdone went too. It took Steel and his merry men 5 miles to get up with the flying 3 and the men who were to be in there at the finish were all together after only 15 miles.

Just beyond Abergarie, Mather had had enough and dropped off, but on the *prime* climb, Clarke took the lead from Proctor in the final few yards. Down the other side they had to pedal like mad to stay upright so fierce was the wind, but once over Kincardie Bridge the course swung and the speed crept up again. On and on they went, faster and faster went the pedals, with everyone along the route shouting encouragement to them. It was Ian Steel, over and over again, up at the front, stirring things up and making them move faster and faster, and it was Steel, Steel, Steel, all the way to the line, and the judges' lives wouldn't have been worth living if they hadn't given him the verdict. Their verdict was inches, but it was, in fact, half-a-wheel, and five were there in Don Wilson, 2nd, Bev Wood, 3rd, Michaux, 4th and Pete Proctor, 5th. Unexplained is the fact that the other 3 didn't even get into the finishing picture, yet got the same time!

STAGE 10.   EDINBURGH TO NEWCASTLE   112 MILES.

Back into dear old blighty today and with only 49 of the original 78 left. According to the dear old 'comic' there was friction between the old Union riders of B.S.A. and the pure League teams. Mind you, the officials were no slouches. One rider did eventually get penalised for the infringements, much to his disgust, but it was obvious that someone, somewhere was stirring the mire, and reckoned that he was working for the League.

It was the flag that dropped, not the penny, and within 1 mile, Con Carr of Ireland was laying in the dust and dirt of the road, nursing a bone fracture in one hand and sundry deep head wounds. When these lads play, they play for keeps!

Although attacks were made frequently, nothing came of them. It was at Galashiels, 33 miles from the start that the first break came, and then it seemed, only by chance. Scales, Maitland and Yeaman eased themselves from their saddles to give their rear-ends a rest, jumped, and surprisingly, didn't get pulled back. The door was open and off they went, just as Bev Wood stopped with a snapped gear cable, and Blair had to stop too with gear trouble. Team-mates Fenwick and Welch dropped out of the back immediately to help out.

The lead 3 got down to it and after about 10 miles they had a lead of 1½ minutes. At Jedfoot Bridge, another 10 miles had sped under their wheels and the lead was now 3½ minutes. Up on the heart-rending climb of Carter Bar they bent their backs in earnest, for both Scales and Maitland were aware of the fact that, now that they had a 4½ minutes lead, it was one or the other of them who would take over the yellow jersey, and that it would all be decided, God willing, on the finishing line.

Yeaman (Pennine) takes the mountain *prime*, and they re-group and get down to the job of increasing their lead. Any animosity, if there ever was any was forgotten in the struggle for supremacy. Behind them, Proctor had gone beserk and had found enough energy to get to the top of Carter Bar for fourth place, and so became 'King of the Mountains' for 1952.

At Belsay, with 15 miles to go, the trio had a lead of 5½ minutes, and they were thrashing the living daylights out of themselves and each other, in an effort to get speed and then more speed. How they worked, throwing in short bursts of speed, sprinting flat out, changing in a short, sharp echelon that was painful even to watch.

They flashed into Claremont Road in line, and first Scales, then Maitland, then Yeaman took the lead, forcing the pace up and up until legs would revolve no faster. Scales' bike wobbles as he gets out of the saddle and over the front wheel to get more push and it took him just ahead of the other two and they hammer on to the line and it was Scales by a length from Yeaman, with Bob Maitland, half-a-length away, 3rd.

It was over 5 minutes later that Ken Russell came in with a big bunch of 34 riders and this means that Les Scales (Sun) took over the *maillot jaune,* with Bob Maitland (B.S.A.) 2nd, Russell 3rd, and Bill Bellamy, the Romford amateur, 4th.

STAGE 11.   NEWCASTLE TO SCARBOROUGH   88 MILES.

It was a dry day, but there were heavy clouds scudding across a near-leaden sky. The day started slowly, with Les Scales proudly wearing the yellow jersey of race leader for the first time. The compact field of 48 ambled along, seemingly not going anywhere in particular, but the pace was being increased gradually.

At Low Fell, Steel and Welch, Viking pair, up bottoms, eased off the front, made daylight and are gone. One hundred, two hundred yards, and then a $\frac{1}{4}$ mile. Behind them the B.S.A. smelt danger, got to the front, and led a charge that was reminiscent of the charge of the Light Brigade. On, and on it went until just after Sedgefield, Steel looked around, sat up, patted Welch on the head and let the bunch catch them. As they were absorbed they gave a cheery grin to the sweat-streaked chasers, and Stan Jones touched a kerb and blew a tyre.

As they scurried through Stockton on Market Day a stray dog took it into its head to run out in front of the bunch and Greenfield gave a sudden swerve to avoid it. 'Tiny' Thomas took evasive action to miss Ian Greenfield, didn't quite make it, and sat down suddenly. Proctor and Newman stopped to help 'Tiny', and quite suddenly there were four B.S.A. men *behind* the bunch.

Opportunities like this come but once and this was enough for Russell who shot off like a ball of fire, and on his rudder went Pottier, Van den Dooren, Fenwick and Charlie Mather. On Buck Brow, Ken pounded 'em into the dust and one by horribly struggling one they dropped off, and at the top, he was on his own.

Ian Steel must have been having a nap for he was still with the bunch. Watch-dog Maitland followed his every movement, but kept glancing back to see if his team-mates were coming up. For a fleeting second his mind wasn't on the job and Steel was away. Moving fantastically fast he caught Russell's 'tail' and went smoothly through Mather, Van den Dooren, Pottier and up to Fenwick, leaving no tell-tale 'wake'. Trevor is made of sterner stuff than the others and where Steel went, Trevor went too.

Yard by thrashing yard, Steel pulled Russell back and at the top of Scaling Dam with 30 miles to go, Ian, still with Trev in tow, caught Ken, who just gave a big grin. Ian gives him a brotherly pat on the back, and the three then got down to some real work.

It was at Butt's Corner that Fenwick blew, and the shattered hulk was left behind, as Steel and Russell really went to town. Across Low Moor they raced, taking turn and turn about, first the giant Steel and then the tiny Yorkshireman, but at Cloughton it was Russell who hung on to Ian's wheel and it seemed as though the end of Ken was in sight.

But what a brilliant job he did! He hung on to that wheel knowing full well that he had all the morrow to recoup his strength, and the 'black' must have descended several times by the way he switched and swerved, but they raced into Scarborough together, and out along the Marine Drive it was Steel in front, virtually towing Ken. The mist seemed to lift from Russell's eyes as he threw everything into a last almighty effort and on the line he took Steel, who had done a tremendous amount of work, by a length,

Back up the road, the speed rose to a crescendo and they were pounding out the rhythm of the chase and counting off the minutes one by one. Bill Bellamy had the lead and took a corner too fast, and shot over a barbed-wire fence and into a field. Team-mates crash-stopped and helped to get him out, and he struggled on to the finish where an examination shows that he has fractured one of his vertebrae, which made it curtains for him.

With the field coming in more than 5 minutes after him Ken Russell now leads by 4 minutes from Scales and Maitland, and the Viking team have pulled up 21 minutes behind the B.S.A. team.

STAGE 12. SCARBOROUGH TO NOTTINGHAM 125 MILES.

Heavy rain clouds scudded over Scarborough on the day off, but everyone was inside making final preparations for the 'run-in'. As it was on this very stage the year before that many had gone off course, the route markers had been out having a field day, and anyone going off course on this day would have to be completely blind.

Russell got his *maillot juane*; the Mayor made a complimentary speech, and off they pedal. Up at Sherburn, Proctor, Don Wilson, Fenwick, Christison and Pottier left the bunch to fend for itself, and at Norton, with 23 miles on the clock, their lead was nearly $1\frac{1}{2}$ minutes.

In the bunch, Russell was safely esconced in a cocoon, and as none of the riders in the 'tearaway' bunch could do him any harm on General Classement he was content to let sleeping dogs lie, and let others do the work.

Of course, he watched Scales and Maitland as his two nearest challengers, and with a side wind and 7 other riders to help them, they should have been able to make a decisive move. At York, the position remained the same, except that the fugitives had a nice lead of 4 minutes.

Across the flats to Selby they trundled not making any impression on the leaders, who managed to race over a level-crossing just as it was about to close. The field was forced to stop, but some climbed over the gates or over the footway carrying their bikes. Michaux (Belgium) and Steel were the first over and, while Michaux dithered as to what to do, Ian shot away on his own. Mather and Newman wait for no man and race after him and the trio soon left the main bunch far behind.

They soon passed Christison, who had death in his legs and, passing through Bawtry, learnt that they were only 2 minutes behind, while at Ollerton they were all but breathing down the backs of the necks of the leaders. They joined forces with only 18 miles to go, and then proceeded to do everything they could to break the group up, and everything was thrown in bar the kitchen sink!

They swung into the Recreation Ground to the cheers of thousands, and again it was Ian Steel that made all the running. Flat out he went, riding like a maniac but forgetting the corner to be negotiated in his haste. Up the grass bank he goes, followed by Alf Newman, and 5 lucky lads went by.

Nothing daunted, he strained at the straps and so fast did he make up ground that he passed 3, but Trev Fenwick (Pennine) got the verdict from Johnny Pottier (Viking) at inches with the redoubtable Steel, 1½ lengths away, 3rd. It was a full minute more before the field came in, which goes to show that they had, at last, got off their bottoms, and it included all the fancied ones, so that Steel was now in 5th position, just under 9 minutes behind Russell.

STAGE 13. NOTTINGHAM TO NORWICH 123 MILES.

This was the dreariest stage of the race. Flat, uninteresting, windless miles rolled across to Norwich, but with less than 10 miles covered, Newman and Bodson (Belgium) were having a private 'tug-of-war' and have gone clear of the field. Soon, a fearsome fivesome in Phillips, Stan Jones, Cook (R.A.F.), Welch and Bougeois (Belgium) had made a date and were hurtling up the road after them.

By Grantham, the original 2 were still away, but the 5 were close behind. Bodson got fed up and dropped back, so Alf sat up and waited for the chasers. The newly-formed group of 6 had only a slight lead, but mile by mile and minute by minute the gap widened.

Chasing groups were forming up and marching off and the main field really began to get worried. So worried in fact that, just before Donnington, they threw everything into one big clean up and had pulled everyone back into one big group. But not for long!

Came a 5 minute 'sit-down' and off went Thomas, Jones, Phillips and Pottier and at Fosdyke, with 52 miles on the clock, they had a slim lead of 20 seconds. Between the 'dyke and Sutton they rustled up more speed and the lead is now 2 minutes. By Kings Lynn it had crept up to 3½ minutes.

A group of 3, Christison, Welch and Yeaman form up as the Three Musketeers, and they sped through Kings Lynn flat out to try and catch the flying 4. Just outside Norwich they made it and all 7 knew by instinct that they would have to fight out the finish.

There was no argy-bargy as round the Ring road they raced and, in the narrow down-hill finishing lane 'Tiny' Thomas won a car-baulked sprint from the 6 others, for the judges withheld any time bonuses, making Thomas the winner, and the other 6 equal second. It was barely 3 minutes later that the main bunch roared in, and the *maillot juane* was still safe on the shoulders of Ken Russell.

STAGE 14.   NORWICH TO LONDON   119 MILES.

It was a watery sun that greeted the 43 riders, and there were only a few of them who had the opportunity of taking Russell's crown from him, but you can be certain that if they could, they would!

After 15 miles, a streak of blue flashes away and it was Don Wilson who was out to spike the big guns and make a name for himself. Swiftly the gap opens. Blair seized his chance, and a Viking rider was away. It took 26 miles of slogging for the bunch to pull them back.

Immediately, away went Aldridge (Romford) and Newman, and at Thetford they had a lead of 1 minute. At Newmarket, Maitland, Scales and Thomas made road, and Russell sensing the danger, goes along for the ride. After 50-odd miles they caught the 2 leaders, and there were 3 B.S.A. men and only one Russell. For long, sweat-raked minutes he had to take on all 3 with Les Scales thrown in for make-weight. Then up came the main bunch with a rush and Ken could breathe again.

They jockeyed for position, yet stayed whole, and it was left to Stan Jones to streak off on his own. As he passed through Royston, he had a 3 minute lead and looked lonely. Behind him, the peloton got off its bottom, and Scales and Maitland take off, only to find Russell was in their 'back pocket', together with the Belgium, Michaux.

At Baldock, Jones was 1½ minutes in front of the four, who now had 3 minutes on the peloton. Stevenage comes at 88 miles, and Jones thankfully joins up with the chasing 4. Then the 'loner', Ken Russell ran out of luck. Through 13 stages he had had a trouble-free ride; no punctures; no mechanical trouble – nothing.

The story of these last 25 miles is like a dream. First the clamping-screw of his left-hand cotterless crank had begun to come loose and on every turn of the pedals there was a sideways play of more than an inch. He was sitting uncomfortably on the back; 'sitting in' someone remarked, but he was, in fact, trying to tighten the screw with his fingers.

He espied a mobile marshal close behind, acting as 'chaperon' and he dropped back and told the marshal his trouble, asking him to get him a spanner. He was never to get it, for just then, *he felt his front tyre softening.* They were now on the outskirts of London at Watford Way, and Ken knew that he would get no help from Les Scales, who was lying second on General Classification, or from Maitland or Jones who were team-mates.

Then began a parody which has no equal in the world of cycle sport, before or since. His one and only hope was Michaux. A Belgian, 'tis true, and 8th on 'General'. He had set his heart on winning a stage of this race and was turning over in his mind the chances when Russell rode up alongside of him. Ken's knowledge of Flemish or French was little, just one or two words, but as they rode along he managed to piece together a sentence, and murmured to Michaux, 'Donnez moi votre bicycle,' pointing anxiously to the loose crank and the softening tyre.

Michaux made up his mind at once, grinned, jumped off his machine, and Ken was off after Scales, Maitland and Jones, while Michaux sat on the kerb patiently changing a tyre and trying to tighten up the loose screw.

Up front, again Ken Russell was in trouble for, while turning a corner he had noticed a crack in the right-hand blade of the Belgian's forks, and there he was again, praying hard to Providence that it would hold to the finish. He sat, ill-at-ease behind the others, knowing full well that he should attack, but not daring to because of the cracked fork.

Through Colney Hatch Lane they raced through cheering thousands, and Ken was now desperately hanging on in the hope that, if all else failed, he could run the last mile or so to the finish. The fork, creaking now under the strain, held and, on the run-in it was Les Scales who took the initiative and swung round the last right-handed bend to beat Ken Russell by 10 lengths, with Bob Maitland third, a further 5 lengths away.

The terrific gamble had paid off, and the 'loner' had made it. For minutes afterwards he wept on Michaux's shoulder when he finally came in. The last stage of this great race had been 'a race apart' with enough 'happenings' to have made the most 'flowery' of us conscious of its greatness.

4: The 'Fighting' Tour

Tour of Britain, 1953
September 6th—19th

Somehow, through the interim period between the '52 Tour and this one, Eddie Lawton, the League 'swash-buckling' fighter and his henchmen had got down to some hard work and had pulled enough strings to make this, the third *Express* Tour of Britain, *officially* recognised by the Union Cycliste International, the world controlling body for cycling.

It must have been over a few dead bodies of 'Union' officials, because never before had the League been recognised, and here were the first moves being made, albeit to climb on a wagon that had been most successful, and on towards 'negotiation' and possible amalgamation.

Of course, this meant that tougher foreign teams were now available, and France, Belgium and Italy had nominated strong teams that would give the 'personalities' with the British 'equipes', such as Russell, Steel, Scales and Maitland, a very good run for their money.

The start had been brought back to London and round at the Cockpit in Hyde Park all the fun of the fair was going on, with last minute preparation, oiling of legs, massaging backs, adjusting back numbers, etc. Team Managers, mechanics, masseurs strutted around, giving a pat here, a word of encouragement there, for these lads were the ones who kept the teams together and happy during this 1,631 miles race.

Out of the sun there was a chilling South-East wind; and no-one wanted to stand around too long, and track suits were zipped up to keep out the breeze. Ian Steel started with a handicap, a burst carbuncle on his right thigh, but it had been well dressed and covered in plaster.

60

Everyone finally got rounded up and they commenced the processional ride from Hyde Park, via Regents Park, Seven Sisters Road, and Ferry Lane to the 'Queen Elizabeth' at Chingford Station. There were massed crowds out to see the riders pass and the whole thing had a tremendous carnival and circus flavour about it.

Professional discipline had already begun in Hyde Park when the Hercules team had signed in late and had been fined 5 shillings each. Everyone prayed that, having dug their heels in, the officials would continue to hand out 'justice' for the rest of the 14 days of racing.

STAGE 1. LONDON (CHINGFORD) TO GREAT YARMOUTH   126 MILES.

After partaking of lunch, the 59 couriers lined up, all set for the gruelling job ahead. Behind them were the mobile marshals, the team and service cars, and overhead hovered a 'publicity' helicopter. There were huge crowds everywhere, up went the flag, then down . . . and away they went.

Out on the Epping road they were strung out like so much colourful washing on a line, and Wisinsky of France had the honour of being first off his bike when his chain unshipped but, with the help of team-mate Geneste, got back on again before the field reached Harlow.

By this time however, the first break had gone. 9 men in Ilsley, Talbot, Jowers, Parkin, Jowett, Bellay, Fenwick, Welch and Brian Robinson had made the break. Only one foreigner was included: Bellay of France, but the Italians in the bunch were alert to the danger and really stirring it up.

At Bishop's Stortford, they hurtled down the hill and Ciancola (Italy) waited for no man and 'bridged that gap' of 600 yards between the bunch and the leaders effortlessly. The 10 worked as one, tremendously hard, and slowly, oh, so slowly, they began to pull away from the main bunch.

Keenahan, (Aspirants 'B') broke a rear spindle and was left behind, but the rest just kept on rolling. At Six Mile Bottom, the fugitives had a lead of 50 seconds, and the Rosslyn Ladies were passed going the other way in their 12 hour *contre le montre*.

Over the undulations to Newmarket the pace was hotted up and by Barton Mills the lead was nearly 2 minutes, and Jowers had 'died the death'. Already they were well ahead of schedule and were soon belting through the feeding station, 4 miles outside of Thetford.

The leaders picked up their musettes alright, but when the bunch came screaming through, Yeaman (Pennine) took a tumble when his 'feed bag' got caught in his front wheel, and Bas. Reeves (Triumph) punctured.

Around 80 miles, Bellay sat up, had a long talk with his Team Manager (they were on the backs of motor-bikes) and dropped back to the main bunch. No explanation, no nothing, just fed up! It was around here that the Italians in the bunch went on the rampage, and throwing everything in, except a spanner, got Gestri and Monti clear, but wily Bev. Wood (Viking) managed to go with them.

And what magnificent effort they put into it! In less than 20 miles they bridge a near 3 minute gap. Through Wymondham it was 1½ minutes and in the next 5 miles they hammered themselves to such an extent they got with the leaders, passing Parkin (Pennine), nearly out on his feet and gone the way of all flesh.

So it was 10 little nigger boys who belted on towards Acle, and all points to Yarmouth. Monti and Ciancola were dishing it out in the lead group, while Bedwell (Hercules) and Wisinsky (France) were doing the same in the bunch, while Chiti (Italy) was doing his darndest to slow them down.

Through the lanes around Caister, the 3 minutes became 2, then one . . . then seconds only, with 7 riders making a break from the peloton, with the main bulk of the field being covered by 50 seconds.

The Italians poised themselves for the kill, positioning themselves nicely, all three at the front. Monti and Ciancola 'go' and Gestri just sat up. Only Wood manages to get round him, and on the line it was Monti from Ciancola by several lengths, with Bev. Wood, third.

STAGE 2. GREAT YARMOUTH TO LEICESTER 142 MILES.

This was really two stages, the first 'innovation' of its kind in any British 'Tour'. Yarmouth to Peterborough as a road race, and

Peterborough to Leicester 'contre le montre'. By doing this it was felt that everyone would be on different times by the end of the day, and thus would be easily identifiable.

They started from the Floral Clock and 2 miles later the race was de-neutralised. As the flag dropped, so Geneste and Baele took off, and Ciancola and Chiti hammered up from the back, and down went Chiti and Ciancola, having hit a spectator. Only a grazed elbow from Ciancola, and with the help of Ciolli they were soon back on, only to find that the two Frenchmen had led the field astray.

It meant another 7 miles on to the stage, and they got back on the right road near Acle. At Norwich, Bedwell (Hercules) Maitland, Steel, Ilsley, Fenwick and Parker had ½ minute on the bunch which was getting restless. More and more got the wanderlust and shot off the front, and at 68 miles there were 29 in the lead group and 29, not all together, behind. Ciolli (Italy) is off the back through sickness and Gestri his mate had stopped to help him. They were to lose 17 minutes on the field.

The sun was hot and drinks were like gold-dust. At the feeding station, two Frenchmen, Bellay and Geneste took everyone by surprise and hared off into the blue. Pandemonium reigned and it was several hectic miles before they were pulled back. As they caught them, Geneste went again, and it was Baele who went with him this time, and Bev. Wood and Guldemont (Belgium), not to be outdone, went with them for a bit of company.

Stan Saunders (Triumph), Les Scales, Johnny Pottier and Ciancola said goodbye to the rest and got up with the leaders. What a group this was, and what a sensation they caused as they pounded through lunch-time crowded Wisbech, with their 1½ minute lead.

Across the Fens they screamed and Ciancola kept looking back for the *maillot jaune* figure of Monti. Every mile was getting faster; no one else was to get up with them, and for the remaining 8 miles nothing could get near or touch this frolicking eightsome.

The finish was stupidly placed, being off the main A.47 road on to the Agricultural Society's grounds, which meant going through a narrow gateway and over a 10ft wide gravel path, followed by a sharp left-hander and then 70 yards of rough, tough grassland.

Ciancola took the stage easily from Scales and Wood, and all in the group moved up on General Classification with Ciancola taking the yellow jersey.

After lunch they still had to face the 39 miles 'time-trial' to Leicester. This is a British 'speciality', but again the continentals showed us the way to go about it by taking 1, 2 and 3, in Guldemont (Belgium); Tamburlini (France) and Ciancola (Italy). This put Ciancola well and truly in the *maillot jaune*.

STAGE 3.   LEICESTER TO LEEDS   134 MILES.

Another fine day heralded the first of the 'mountain' climbs, and the 'off' from Leicester was but a preliminary in the skirmishes that were to follow. The long climb of the Via Gellia saw numberless attacks that broke the field up into 5 groups, but at the top they suddenly all became as 1.

At 50 miles, 15 likely lads shot out from cover, got themselves into some semblance of order, and started making the running. None of the leading lights were there and so, at 58 miles, back they came. But not so Norman Yeaman. As the front of the bunch reached the back of the lead group he sprinted away, and after him went Ciolli and Baele (France). Doug Petty (Wilson) made a superb effort to 'bridge that gap', and then there were 4.

'Leave them out there to die' seemed to be the order of the day, 'cos none of them were really anything 'special' but, on the ups and downs between Buxton and Chapel-en-le-Frith they steadily built up an impressive lead. Behind them at 1 minute, a group including Brian Robinson (Ellis-Briggs) Russell; Jowers (Aspirant 'A'), Garvey, Mathieu and Bedwell were making ground.

On the climb before Glossop, the break-maker Yeaman dropped back with gear trouble. Came the steep, steep climb of Holme Moss and Ciolli took it in his stride, reaching the top 20 seconds in front of Baele and 35 seconds in front of Doug Petty. Less than 1 minute passed and over came Jowers and then came the rest, one by one grunting, puffing and struggling.

Down, down they skimmed, with the leading 3 getting away with murder as they cut corner after corner, while behind them, man after man crashed, punctured or had 'death in their legs'. Ciancola, Gestri, Geneste, Ilsley, Reeves, Buttle and Tamburlini

Ken Russell, the loner, coming in second on the last stage of the 1952 Tour. This was the stage where his bottom bracket came loose, he changed bikes and then found that one of the fork blades was cracked

Bev Wood, the Viking rider, being handed up his musette (feed bag) by his manager Bobby Thom during the Tour of Britain, 1953

The 1952 'Tour' riders on their first hill prime

all took tumbles or punctured, and the first-aid and service vehicles had a rare old time.

Ciancola's arm was puffed up like a balloon, but he kept going. Traffic lights made more delays for some, and got penalties for 'failing to halt' for others. The lead 2 kept moving, for Petty had by this time been passed by the hungry wolves reaching out for the leaders.

For 30 long, hot and weary miles, these 2 stayed away, then Ciolli cracked wide open, and Baele virtually carried him for a further 3 miles. Looking round on a long straight stretch he saw the hounds moving in for the kill at speed and, sprinting away, left the deflated Ciolli to his fate.

Tiny Bedwell was in there, whipping them up to a frenzy, but still it wasn't enough to catch Baele. Every mile saw his Team Manager telling him that he had only 'one kilometre to go', and every mile seemed to see him slowing to the point of being caught.

Came the moment of truth and, summoning up every last ounce of strength left in him, he hurtled on to the finish to win by 52 seconds from the flying Bedwell and Bruno Monti, a wonderful ride that had pulled all the stops. Ciancola finished nearly six minutes down, and so the *maillot jaune* went on to the shoulders of Henri Guldemont of Belgium.

STAGE 4.   LEEDS TO SCARBOROUGH   104 MILES.

'Ciancola and Gestri have abandoned' said their Team Manager, and it appeared that the erst-while race leader had a severe cold and his arm was troubling him. It was dry and bright, and the humidity had dropped considerably as they trundled merrily out of Leeds.

This was to be another day of aggressive riding and there were 5 miles of 'sorting out' and then 7 men got clear. The main bunch sensed danger and pounded out the rhythm of the chase but, at Tadcaster, 3 more made their move, and the leaders now numbered ten. The chase reached its height and as they pounded towards York, word came back that the lead group had a lead of two minutes.

The field slowed suddenly, and 14 men took off, loosened themselves from the grip of the bunch and chased, and chased, and

C   65

chased. It was a hard chase and it was not until Barmby-on-the-Moor that they finally made contact with the fugitives, and the front bunch became 24 with one foreign rider, Mathieu (Belgium) therein.

The yellow jersey was behind, and they belted out the first 50 miles in 1 hour 57 minutes, and there was no sign of a move from Guldemont, the *maillot jaune*. Attack is followed by attack at the front and Bellamy and Thomas got away to a short-lived break. Back in the main bunch, Gestri (Italy) had 'died', and that was the end of Italy's hopes in the team race.

Into a headwind they ploughed, and continued with their furious onslaught. Jowett (Viking) goes, and was left out there to take a beating, and came back. Saunders, Fenwick and Parker gained a few yards on the run-in, and it was these vital yards that gave the verdict to Parker by 2 seconds from Saunders (Triumph) and Fenwick (Wearwell), four seconds behind. There were 23 British riders in the first 24, and the continental domination has been broken. Johnny Pottier (Wearwell) was the official race leader from Bev. Wood of the Viking 'equipe' by 15 seconds.

STAGE 5. SCARBOROUGH TO NEWCASTLE 136 MILES.

After a good day's rest by the sea the 56 riders left in lined up without complaint to 'carry coals to Newcastle'. Dark clouds scudded across a lowering sky, the sun was blotted out and rain threatened.

Off into open country and the wind was now howling at near gale force. It swept at them from the side, from the front, from the rear. As they tackled the climbs over the Yorkshire Moors it was mostly in their faces, but eleven men took it all in their stride, left the bunch and were away on their own.

11 miles went by and they had a lead of 20 seconds. By Ruswarp, 19 miles, they had a lead of 1 minute, and in there was *maillot jaune* Pottier; Geneste and Bellay (France); Monti; Maitland; Bedwell; Garvey; Greenfield; Bev Wood and Brian Robinson. It was a good group to be with, and they were to fight out this storm together for nearly 6½ hours.

At 30 miles their lead was given as 2½ minutes with Grondelaers and Guldemont, Belgium in between at 1 minute 25 seconds. At

38 miles, these 2 were back in the bunch and the leaders were given 3 minutes. The slopes of Scaling Dam offered no shelter and it was struggle, struggle, toil and trouble all the way.

Attack followed attack in the bunch behind, but to no avail. The front bunch showed no mercy, but each one had been nurtured with the knowledge that they daren't break up in the conditions that appertained. They just had to consolidate, to conserve their own and each other's energy so that all would be intact at the finish.

They jumped fire hoses in Scorton, and after West Auckland they tackled the long ascent of Tow Law and the gusts of wind reached a new ferocity. It was 'Iron Man' Bedwell who, by superhuman effort took the prime from Frank Garvey (Aspirant) by 10 lengths and then, as they dropped the 10 miles down to Corbridge, the road swung in an easterly direction, and shoulders were eased back, and up went the speed at once.

Up and up it soared into the 30's. Where before they had nearly crawled along, now they flogged themselves to the point of no return; where Bellay (France) was terribly sick and cried 'enough'. Behind them the B.S.A. men were getting niggled at their 5 minute deficit, but there was nothing they, or anyone else could do about it.

As the line came in sight it was Talbot, Bedwell's team-mate who let fly, taking the left hand side. The others, thinking he was making his effort went with him, but Bedwell, who knew a thing or two, took the right hand side and, keeping well into the gutter, sprinted away to win by lengths.

Over 7 minutes later most of the field scurried in, but Bedwell had moved up to 2nd place on General, only 4 seconds behind Johnny Pottier.

STAGE 6. NEWCASTLE TO GLASGOW 151½ MILES.

The dark clouds had gone and there was sun and a light, light breeze for the start. Pottier had the yellow jersey but it was a very uneasy one for there were a number of riders close behind. Out of Barrack Road they pedalled with whistles and shouts from thousands of 'Geordies' and once the race became de-neutralised it was Guldemont, Ilsley, Baele and Bellay who slipped the leash.

With 150 miles in front of them, the others were content to see

THE TOUR OF BRITAIN - 1953

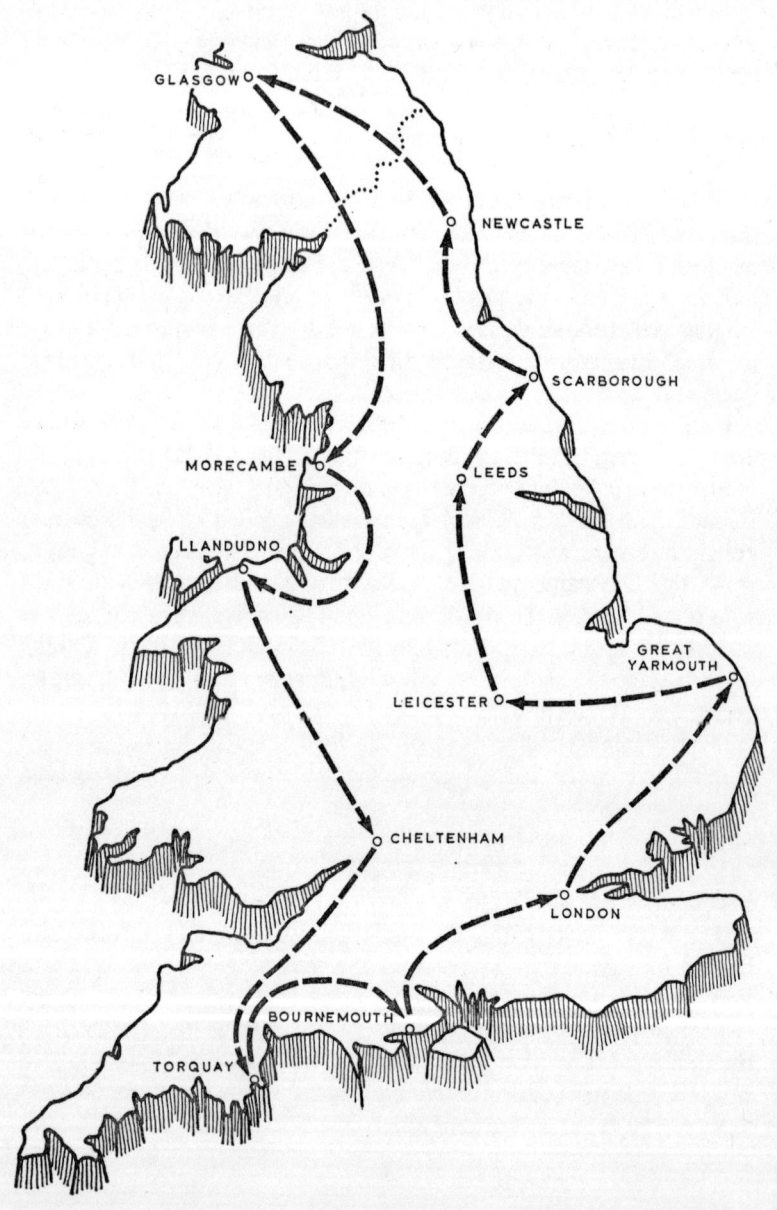

them go. After all, they had Carter Bar and Peebles hills in front of them. They'd come back of course, once the bunch had got settled in and the day's stage really got under way! But at Kirk-whelpington, they had begun to get a bit worried for the flying 4 had a neat 5 minutes in hand. It was here that Bellay's gear cable snapped . . . and then there were 3!

The bunch were a bit more happier when they heard the news, but up the 10 mile climb of Carter Bar the 3 kept at it, and the wind blew at them across the moorland. Up and up, getting farther and farther away from the *peloton,* and at the *prime* it was Ilsley winning the £15 prize from Guldemont and Baele, and the main bunch is at 9 minutes.

Over the top they hustled and got down to it again. Down through Jedburgh and St. Boswells, and the lead had dropped to 7 minutes. Their feeding time over and on they hammer to Peebles, where the lead was 11 minutes, and this produced pandemonium in the main bunch.

Ian Steel and Wisinsky had shot off in pursuit, but Bedwell and Parker hammered the rhythm and pulled them back, and the break was nullified. However, the up-life of speed in the main bunch had brought the lead tumbling down to 6 minutes, but Monti of Italy was out on his own at 5 minutes.

Mile after solitary mile he hurried on, pulling back the minutes on the leaders until he was within 3 minutes of them. He chased anything and everything that moved in an effort to get more speed, but it was all for nothing for the *peloton,* with the bit between its teeth, pounded out time and caught him at Hamilton with only 12 miles to go.

The leaders were told of the falling minutes, and they stepped up their speed and Ilsley was 'slipped' on a short hill only 20 miles from the finish, and was soon absorbed by the chasers.

Up at the front, Guldemont had made no mistake as to who was to have the stage, for he won by 3 lengths from Baele. On the run-in, it was Steel who was telling everyone to watch out for the tram-lines. Out of Hamilton, he and Wisinsky (France) took off and by Cambuslang, it was Steel who had fallen a victim to his own tram-lines and Wisinsky was on the way to getting third place, $2\frac{1}{2}$ minutes down. Bedwell took 4th place and the yellow jersey by *4 seconds* from Pottier, a reversal of the previous day.

Cycling's 'Circus'

STAGE 7. GLASGOW TO MORECAMBE 164 MILES.

There were only 22 seconds between the first and fourth man on General Classification at this, the halfway stage. It was another fine September Sunday, and the traffic was already heavy as they lined-up for the off. 'Iron Man' Bedwell got his *maillot jaune* and away they went out of George Square.

Everyone wanted to have a go, but remarkably few got away with it. Chitti and Doug Petty, were the first to succeed, but within 3 miles, 'bang-bang' and they were back in the fold. Others tried time and time again, but the leaders were obviously not having any.

At Abington, on one of the long climbs, 6 men thought that 39 miles was enough to be all together and erupted from the bunch. Monti; Thomas; Welch; Maitland; Greenfield and Petty had formed a leading group. Over the Beattock Hills they thrashed and lead by ½ minute, and by Beattock village the lead had increased by 2 minutes.

The field got stroppy and by the time 65 miles had gone by they had pulled them all back except Greenfield, who had gone hunting on his own. He was obviously after the Border Prime and made it with a full 3 minutes to spare.

Carlisle was packed with people and here, Don Wilson (Aspirant A), Fenwick (Wearwell), Syd Wilson (Wilson), Ilsley, Parker (Hercules) and Wisinsky went searching for Greenfield. They caught him 3 miles down the road, and 2 miles further on were duly caught themselves by Bedwell, Thomas and Talbot. Even before Penrith came in sight, the entire field came belting up all around them.

Yeaman and Wisinsky shot off, prepared to do battle for the Shap Fell *prime,* but Bedwell was there, warming things up for the fray, and with Parker he hammered out a rhythm that could not be denied and took the lolly by 10 lengths from Ken Russell (Ellis-Briggs).

The field were now split into 2, and 21 men raced down towards Morecambe, scaring the daylights out of the motorists they passed in doing so. Wisinsky and Bellay lead the fray, together with Ray Holliday (Aspirant) who wouldn't work with them and so, by Kendal, they were as one. The steam-roller sped towards the sea, many of the cars they passed joining in.

70

21 riders thundered along the promenade together, and it was Maitland (B.S.A.) who scrambled into the lead. Tight in the middle of the bunch sat Bedwell and it seemed impossible for him to get out. He did a bit of juggling with his 'bars and, swinging right round to the right of the hurtling bunch, threw himself and his bike towards the line. The huge crowds saw the tiny figure blaze into a blurr of speed and on his wheel was Monti. As they screamed on towards the line, Bedwell caught Bob Maitland and, with 20 yards to go, got by, and Monti was trying to get up there and contest it. Dave Bedwell thrashed at the pedals and made it, with Monti in his slip-stream, and a very dazed Maitland, third. Behind them, the whole bunch, travelling at lightning speed, hammered across the line in a solid, heaving mass.

Bedwell's timing had been just right, for the bonuses won during the day now put him 1½ minutes ahead of Pottier.

STAGE 8. MORECAMBE TO LLANDUDNO 125 MILES.

This was to be Bedwell's black day, for he was to drop the biggest clanger of all time and drop from 1st to 15th place on this stage. It started out well enough, with a bit of sky-larking about at the start, the day was fine, and he had the *maillot jaune*. It is said that the B.S.A. team outsmarted him, but I'm sure that it was a combination of circumstances that were well beyond his control.

As the flag dropped, away went Les Scales, Viv Bailes (Aspirants) and 'Tiny' Thomas and they very soon had a lead of 2 minutes. With the long drag down through the black country through Preston, Wigan and Warrington no-one was worrying much, probably because they thought the traffic would be a deterrent anyway.

By Euxton, the 3 had built up a lead of 5 minutes and the pundits in the bunch cried 'enough'. Assault after assault was made, and still Bedwell sat at the back working out, with Buttle, tactics for the day. Very suddenly, 14 men got away and by the time Bedwell had realised what had happened and had worked his way to the front, the 14 were almost out of sight.

Then there happened the saddest saga of all in stage racing. The yellow jersey wearer, out in the cold, and bashing his head against a brick wall. Although Bedwell, Buttle and two Frenchmen pulled out every trick in the book, it was a losing battle, for no-one, but no-one would help them, because they all had teammates up front. The four worked like maniacs, working themselves to a virtual standstill.

Up front, it was all happening; Fenwick (Wearwell) went out with a puncture; Greenfield (Wearwell) had gear trouble; Maitland punctured but team-mate Newman gave him his bike.

At the feeding station, 62 miles, the race leaders were *10 minutes* down and it was all over, bar the shouting. They steam-rollered on along the Frodsham By-pass, and Clarke (Aspirant) took off just 200 yards from the Border *prime,* and getting it, kept going. Nobody bothered much until they realised that there was a hill *prime* 2 miles up the road, and then it was too late. Clarke took that as well!

At the back, Bedwell was taking a hammering of a lifetime, and as the main bunch split, so poor Dave just couldn't take any more and went along for the ride. Pottier who was 2nd on General was there too, and although he did his best, the bunch he was with finally dropped the 'Iron Man' who was by now a sorry sight.

The leaders, having got over the climb, got together, friendly like, and belted down towards Llandudno. By St. Asaph they had 15 minutes on Bedwell, and at Colwyn Bay, 20 minutes, and over the last few miles they increased this by a further 2 minutes.

They certainly gave the crowds their money's worth as they flashed up to the finishing line, and Clive Parker (Hercules) got the verdict by 2 lengths from Les Wilson (Pennine) with Les Scales (Wearwell) six lengths away third. With Brian Robinson classified 'equal 9th' the *mallot jaune* was now his, with Bob Maitland less than $1\frac{1}{2}$ minutes behind, with Guldemont 3rd and Baele 4th. Johnny Pottier came in 14 minutes 3 seconds behind the winner and dropped to 10th place, while Bedwell ambled in with 10 more luckless ones and dropped to 15th position.

STAGE 9. LLANDUDNO TO CHELTENHAM 160 MILES.

There had been cold winds and freezing rain on the rest day, but many were the tactics that had been worked out, and here it was,

Gordon Thomas, the overall winner of the 1953 Tour of Britain, being chaired at Wembley as the results were announced

At Ripon on Stage 4, Les Scales, Wearwell, leads Henri Guldemont (Belgium) and Arthur Ilsley (BSA) during the 1954 Tour of Britain

Ken Russell leads, Tour de France fashion, in the 1955 Tour of Britain

the ninth stage with the sun shining down and this mass of brilliant colour.

Behind them was the last rest day, and 4 days of hard riding lay ahead of them. 45 riders were left in and were gathered for the official send-off from Pier Road and, as in stage races everywhere, more than a bit of bantering was going on.

The Hercules team were determined to get Dave Bedwell back up there somehow and every effort was made to this effect. They controlled the bunch to such an extent that every break was pulled back until the climb out of Conway Falls, and then Bedwell jumped, and just sprinted away. Only 3 men could get with him—Greenfield, Les Wilson and Arthur Ilsley. The rest of the Hercules team formed up in front and let no one past and by the time Bedwell took the 4 over the top, they had a lead of 2 minutes.

Over the hills and far away, and down through Whittington and Shrewsbury the speed rose to a crescendo, with the sky darkening and clouding up fast. First, a gentle drizzle of rain fell, then heavy showers and finally a torrential downpour that went on and on and on. After 90 miles came Cressage Hill and, despite the fact that the road was now like a river, Bedwell, looking like a drowned rat, took this one and the lead on the King of the Mountains. Greenfield was just behind and their lead was $3\frac{3}{4}$ minutes.

By the time the main field comes over most of the storm had passed, and Baele was getting a push from the rest of his team-mates. Eventually he got tailed off, but the whole French team worked like mad and got him back.

Johnny Welch went through Kidderminster like an express train, and for 15 long, cold, wet and lonesome miles he thundered on, pulling back the four leaders. With 30 miles still to go, at Worcester, he made it, went straight to the front and started to pour on the power. From being only $1\frac{1}{4}$ minutes in the lead at Kidderminster, they had $4\frac{1}{2}$ minutes at Tewkesbury, and it was only on the final downhill miles that the *peloton* managed to pull some back, and we were all now in golden sunshine.

Behind them, Chiti was pushing Monti, and several dead ducks went out through the back. Sore rumps were going to be very much in evidence, for grit was being thrown up all the time, and the mechanics would have to spend many hours cleaning the bikes.

Art. Ilsley tried a long one on the run in, but they did not even bother with him. All eyes were on Bedwell and he did not disappoint them. A couple of dummies, then up, out of the saddle he went, and that was the last they saw of him until the other side of the finishing line. Les Wilson followed him in, followed by Ian Greenfield, Johnny Welch and Ilsley in that order, and it was another 3½ minutes before the next man in, Talbot, crossed the line.

The 'Iron Man's' little ditty had pulled him up to 12th place overall, which really was not a lot of consolation for a gallant attempt.

STAGE 10. CHELTENHAM TO TORQUAY 152 MILES.

A huge crowd saw them off from the Queen's Hotel, and on the outskirts of the town away they went and already there were plenty of attacks and counter-attacks. At the *prime* just after Stroud, which Bedwell took, the field were all together except for Stan Jones (B.S.A.) who had a spot of nasal catarrh. Bedwell was making certain of the 'Mountains' prize, and he just didn't bother to fight every inch of the way – he just pulverised them!

Monti and Guldemont threw in short bursts of speed and got a lead, followed by Newman and Wood, but at Pennsylvania with only 38 miles gone, the bunch had them back and ready for chastisement.

Men began popping off the front like ping-pong balls. First Wisinsky, then Iowers, then Don Wilson. Behind them, another three for a game of tennis had formed up in Johnny Welch, Chiti and Frank Garvey (Aspirant), and as they came up to Shepton Mallet, the heavens opened, a thunderstorm broke and the roads were flooded in seconds.

Up the hill out of Mallet the 6 squelch their sloppy way and form up, shaking the water out of their ears and getting down to the essentials. At Glastonbury they had a lead of 2 minutes, and the swish of the board-hard tyres only adds to the stillness that was behind them.

On they pounded, looking round on the long straight stretches, yet seeing no man and, just before Taunton, Wisinsky punctured. Oh, well! Perhaps he would have lived to fight another day, but, so fast did he change that, only 3 miles the other side of Wellington and he was back and hammering the others, and they now had a lead of 8½ minutes.

Out on those steep climbs between Pinhoe and Newton Abbott, Welch was taking a real, right pounding and Wisinsky and Chiti saw this and attacked. The three Aspirants took a real right one-two, but came back time and again for more. It's a neck and neck struggle and Frank Garvey just can't take any more, and out through the back he goes.

They left the hulk behind and there was only Ron Jowers, Don Wilson, Chiti and Wisinsky left, and Chiti tried every Italian dodge that he knew, throwing in everything except 'Il Duce'. He produced, from out of nowhere a tremendous sprint, and it was only the Don (Wilson) who could hold him. Wisinsky and Jowers got left way behind, and then poor old Ron went and punctured.

'Dead-head' Ron borrowed a clubman's bike and dashed the mile or so to the finish to get fourth place and a minute penalty for using a machine that hadn't been tested by the examiners.

But out in front it had been Chiti, Chiti, bang, bang and poor Don Wilson got the rough end of the stick and 2nd place into the bargain. Wisinsky slid in half a minute later, followed by Ron Jowers, and then in came the big bunch, and it was all over for the day.

STAGE 11. TORQUAY TO BOURNEMOUTH 115 MILES.

Sunshine greeted us, and we greeted it! From Beacon Quay we went coast-wise through Honiton and Dorchester to Bournemouth. We didn't know it but, once again, the pattern of the race was to alter and change completely and left us literally gasping.

A scrambling, rambling, fighting field crosses Shaldon Toll Bridge at 8 miles and battle was just about to commence. Less than 12 miles from the start as the field hurriedly pass through Dawlish, four men slipped away, followed at a short interval by three others. Of these, Clarke just could not take the hammering, and dropped back.

There were 6 men out in the clear – Seel (Viking), Pottier and Scales (Wearwell), Parker (Hercules) and Thomas and Ilsley (B.S.A.). An odd-assorted bunch maybe, but at Exminster they had a minute lead, and none of them were less than 5½ minutes down on the race leader, Brian Robinson. There was no air of a do-or-die struggle, and at Honiton they were still *very* insecure, for the lead was now only 58 seconds.

The 22 miles from Honiton to Crewkerne are fairly hard, 'tis true, but they took 4 minutes out of the bunch over this stretch. Another 2 miles and the lead was 6 minutes and Clive Parker (Hercules) was the race leader. Only then it seemed, was it realised that they all had a chance to make a name for themselves, but it was Parker that ran into bad luck.

A nut came loose on his gear and he stopped to change machines with the service vehicle. 'Tiny' Thomas saw his chance, sprang up to giant size suddenly and took off, together with Scales, Pottier and Ilsley. Seel of Viking, dropped back (goodness knows why) to help Parker of Hercules.

The 4 made the hills to Dorchester look like pimples, and the lead was now a fantastic *ten minutes*! They scurried through Bere Regis with 12 minutes in hand, and it seemed that the impossible can sometimes happen!

The *peloton* cut the time slightly but that was all, on the run-in. Scales and Thomas had 'slipped' Pottier and Ilsley with 2 miles to go and pounded it out into Kings Park, with Thomas getting the verdict by a gnat's whisker, with Pottier third, and Ilsley fourth.

It was 9 minutes and 58 seconds later that Frank Seel and Clive Parker rode in, and just over 14 minutes after Thomas had crossed the line, Bedwell led in the charge of the other warriors, and on General Classification it was 'Tiny' Thomas, 1st; Les Scales, 2nd; Johnny Pottier, 3rd, and Brian Robinson, 4th.

STAGE 12. BOURNEMOUTH TO LONDON 121 MILES.

The only rider who might have been happy at the start of this, the last stage, was perhaps Dave Bedwell. After all, he had the 'King of the Mountains' sewn up and in his pocket, and he was to come out of the 'Tour' with more money than the actual winner!

The air was a bit tense as they moved off from the Pavilion Forecourt, and the sight of the 5 B.S.A. men across the front of the field told everyone that they were taking no chances. Up the road, the pace hotted up and at 12 miles there was a 'Road Up' sign and Monti took off with a nice friendly hand-sling from team-mate Chiti, but with the full pack of the B.S.A. men behind him.

They caught him, and the field slowed up, and Talbot and Jowers crashed and ate dirt. Brian Robinson threw in everything but they just would not let him, or anyone else go. Don Wilson got dropped, but by dint of hedge-hopping along the following cars got back on.

Trev. Fenwick got tailed off along the Romsey By-pass, suffering from the effects of his earlier efforts during the week for his team. At Ower, 33 miles, Henri Guldemont attacked, slowed, attacked again and was away. With him went Newman who just would not work and back they came.

The A.30 *prime* was won by Les Wilson, but he just hadn't the inclination to keep going. Through the feeding station they ambled, eating, drinking and getting down once more for more work. The pace is fast and at the Basingstoke By-pass, Maitland, Ilsley, Holliday and Don Wilson had a twenty second lead. Ian Steel punctured and was back in less than a mile. Wisinsky punctured and was back within 100 yards – s'fact! Parkin and Petty went out through the back, and waved goodbye.

At Sunningdale, 91 miles, Pottier and Clarke attacked, but before Chertsey was reached they were back in the net. Brian Robinson takes a powder and got a 10 second lead and remained out there until after Chertsey Bridge, when he was suddenly surrounded by three B.S.A. men.

There were less than 20 miles to go, so no-one was going to make it. They pedalled along singing songs and waving to the crowds. Along the Great Chertsey Road; down the Great West Road, up Hanger Lane and into the North Circular Road. They took up the whole dual carriageway now and it was Grondelaers (Belgium) who slipped away up Neasden Lane to take the last stage of this 'Tour of Britain' by just 4 seconds from Dave Bedwell, who outsprinted Monti (Italy) for 3rd place.

The field came in with 'Tiny' Thomas in the middle, and he acknowledged the crowd's cheers by taking both hands off the handlebars, which promptly copped him a £5 fine, for a breach of the B.L.R.C's Regulations.

And so, it was all over. Gordon 'Tiny' Thomas won, and promptly announced his retirement from the cycling scene; Les

Scales was again second, with John Pottier, team-mate of Wear-well, 3rd. Wearwell very deservedly got the team race, and 'Iron-man' Bedwell was the 1953 'King of the Konks'.

As I said before, it was all over . . . but not quite. The game was still being played, albeit politically, and not in the field.

5: The 'Tour de Tamburlini'

Tour of Britain 1954
June 6th—19th

The 1954 'Tour of Britain' had been a long time in negotiation. It seemed that the sponsors were not prepared to make any major decision one way or the other, and although it was finally approved this was to be the last *Express* Tour.

The race was being started on the Whitsun week-end from the 'kipper' town of Great Yarmouth. The pattern was much the same as before, except that this year there were teams of 6 riders as against 5 heretofore. Italy, France and Belgium were there, perhaps with not such strong riders, but they were couriers who had considerable knowhow. All the British teams this year were sponsored, so that this meant for the first time that no 'pure' amateurs were competing.

It is true that many lessons had been learned trom past mistakes, but the problem of judging still remained the same and again only 5 Judges' names appeared on the panel, all of them doubling up with other jobs.

Being the middle of the British holiday season, Great Yarmouth had been decorated overall, and the Wellington Pier was crammed to bursting point as literally hundreds tried to get a glimpse of the riders. The usual last minute 'panic' was on; one had left his favourite racing socks in his bag; another had the touch of the shudders and was having his back massaged; several were looking vacantly into space, even with all the hub-bub about them, and even more sloped-off to 'spend a penny'.

It happens in all stage races, for those last minutes of freedom before the flag goes down for the first time are sheer agony. Nerves, brought to their highest pitch through hours of inactivity,

79

scream out for release. The mind boggles at the thought of the hundreds of miles that lie ahead. The worry of how you'll shape up to all this gives you the jitters. All in all, it is a wonder that any 'Tourman' ever starts at all for he is virtually, at this moment, a physical wreck, albeit a highly trained one.

Drop that flag and let him get away, and he becomes a physical specimen among athletes that has few equals. They have spent months training for this event, and with the 'off' they take up the challenge, for it is a challenge to every rider in the race, and academic exercise to pit his skill, his craft, his years of knowledge of the bike game, his courage and determination against the supreme problem of all who ride a 'Tour' – survival to win.

From hotel windows hung many a spectator, some in danger of toppling out. From the publicity helicopter above came a steady 'plop-plop' as the blades revolved. Riders scrambled to their feet on this sunny, but windy morning. The flag was raised and fluttered gaily in the breeze. Wheels started to turn slowly and suddenly there were nearly 1,500 miles of pedalling in front of them.

STAGE 1. GREAT YARMOUTH TO LINCOLN 128 MILES.

Jimmy Saville was out in front, telling all and sundry what the race was all about and, by the time the convoy broke town, they were already hard at it. There were virtually no hills on this stage, so that you could call it one for the sprinters. But the 7 likely lads who had left the bunch were Ilsley, Brian Robinson, Greenfield, Talbot, Parker, Bev Wood and Erio Plassa of France. They worked hard and as the miles mounted up so their lead fluctuated between 1 and 2 minutes.

Nearing Swaffham, Dave Bedwell punctured and was a study of muscular synchronisation as his short legs pumped up and down, and threw in short bursts of speed that got him back to the bunch. Not only back, mark you, but through and out the other side, and with new team-mate Freddy Krebs to catch the fugitives at Kings Lynn.

The bunch, including the French, began to turn on the heat and just before Long Sutton, they were all back like one big happy family. But not for long, for Mercier (France) raced away on his own, and stayed that way for many a long mile and, just outside Sutterton as he was tiring, away went Bezamet (French hero of the 1952, Tour of Mexico) and Eugene Tamburlini.

They picked up Mercier on the way, grovelling a bit by now, but they sheltered him until he regained his strength. Up hammered a hand-picked bunch in Pottier, Robinson, Talbot, Joe Christison (Viking) and Jomaux (Belgium), and then the real work began.

No quarter was asked, and none given, and everyone gave their all; just outside Sleaford, Joe Christison (who was racing for the first time in the money ranks), Dennis Talbot and Georges Jomaux said goodbye with the real 'death in their legs'.

By now Arthur Bronckaert was on his way to hospital, having crashed and brought down compatriot, Henry Guldemont. Out of the back of the bunch too, though crashes, have gone Alec Taylor, Ken Russell, Len Wade (Gnutti-Cinelli) and Yvan Corbusier (France).

Up at the front the Frenchmen were having a field day, chopping Pottier and Robinson, so that they didn't know which way was which. It was Tamburlini of the high gear that belted through, taking Mercier on his wheel, allowing him, right at the last moment, to go through between Pottier and Bezamet to take the stage.

Only a photograph came to the rescue of the Judges that day, and their verdict was a dead-heat for second place, with Tamburlini, 4 lengths down, 4th, and Robinson, 10 lengths down, 5th, *but all with the same time.*

Just over 2 minutes later, the field began to trickle in, and of the 50 starters, 49 made it to the line. It had been a hard day's racing, which had given France, 1st, 2nd and 4th places and first in the Team race.

STAGE 2. LINCOLN TO MANCHESTER   90 MILES.
The day dawned chilly with a heavy overcast sky, and there was the promise of a headwind, to boot. There would be no 'fun' today, for the flat of the Fens was left behind and we climbed across the Pennines, including Owler Bar and the Snake Pass.

Germain Mercier was helped on with the *maillot jaune* of the race leader by the Mayor of Lincoln, and it was already damp as they ambled their way out from The Brayford North. Out of town they let 'em go, and as they crossed the flats of Lincolnshire, the heavens opened to the extent of breaking anyone's ardour who was thinking of making a break.

They huddled together, seemingly for comfort, but there's danger of crashing with the bunch and a break did go, six in number, but they were brought back before 10 miles were covered. As they re-grouped off shot Joe Christison and Maitland (B.S.A.) and through Darlton they had a lead of 15 seconds and then a level-crossing gate closed. Of course, the bunch caught them, and then they patiently waited for 6 minutes in the pouring rain while three trains went through, including the Flying Scotsman.

Once the gates opened, off they went, splashing their way through giant puddles and still managed to cover 22 miles in the first hour. Pryor's tyre went off with a bang, and a mile later Alec Taylor was dropped from the bunch. The riders ploughed on through the huge puddles of water on the road, spraying anything and everyone in sight.

As they pedalled on, the route got harder, and through the gusty rain squalls, hills could be seen in the distance. Near Bleak House, Bedwell and Robinson took time out, and set the rest of the field alight. Out of the back came Don Wilson (Gnutti-Cinelli), then Pugi (Italy), while up front, the mighty 2 were handing out a beating.

Across the rugged, wild, Derbyshire Moors, through Hathersage and Bamford they hammered, and behind them the bunch lost Amelynck and Corbusier of Belgium; at the foot of the Snake Pass, Arthur Ilsley (B.S.A.) took an almighty 'packet', as did Tognaccini of Italy.

The tandem got caught on the 9-mile climb of the Snake, and at the top it was Freddy Krebs in the lead, followed by Tamburlini, Pottier, Mitchell (Wearwell) and Ken Joy (Hercules). Then up came 5 more in Robinson, Bedwell, Steel, Jowett and Stan Jones. Clive Parker came up like a 'dose of salts' and went through the second 5 and up to the leaders, and so, on the very slippery descent there were 5, chasing 6.

Down, down they hurtled and then skimmed through Glossop, and on they went, down, down towards Manchester. The water scudded from their wheels, while overhead a watery sun peeped round the sides of black clouds. Krebs had near heart-failure as he found his chain choking up with grit from the road, but up came manager Tom Saunders with an oil-can, and the emergency was soon over.

Joy, Parker and Krebs got together and it was a joy to watch as, ere long, Freddy tried a long one, Joy and Parker formed up at the front, and it was all over bar the shouting. Into Fallowfield Track Krebs hurtled, and once round on the cinder track (as the cycling track was too wet!) to take the stage by 6 seconds from Tamburlini, with Ken Mitchell (Wearwell) a further 2 seconds away, 3rd.

It was Johnny Pottier who now had the yellow jersey on his broad shoulders, but Tamburlini was only 6 seconds behind. The French still had the team lead, but there were only 59 seconds between them and the Hercules mob.

STAGE 3. MANCHESTER TO HARROGATE 75 MILES.

The weather had improved by the time they left Manchester, so they all put their umbrellas away and it was at Debsdale Park that they let them go. 18 miles away was Holme Moss, rearing its ugly head 1,700 ft up into the sky, and it was here that the Frenchmen made for.

From Mottram, there were only 3 riders in it! Tamburlini, Mercier and our own Brian Robinson. What a truly magnificent performance these 3 put up! What a climb it was, and what a cheer went up when Brian beat the two 'froggies' to the *prime* point and gained points in the 'King of the Mountains' prize.

They dropped like stones down to Holmfirth, and then it was just a matter of pedalling and keeping away. The Frenchmen tried time and time again to shed Robinson, but he had had a hard schooling and they couldn't do it. Bit and bit, turn and turn about, sustaining 24 m.p.h. and more, and they kept this up for some 40 odd miles.

At Garforth, with 23 miles only to do, and with nearly 3 minutes in hand, the level-crossing gates closed. They were stopped and not allowed to climb over the gates. They waited, and waited, what must have seemed hours, but was, in reality, only 2½ minutes and, when the train slowly puffed by and out of sight, they found that their lead had been knocked down to a mere 28 seconds.

Most would have sat up and let the bunch catch them – but not these 3. Again they got down to it, but now the *peloton* had got off its bottom and there was a bunch of 12 chasing them. In this group were Maitland, Ilsley, Newman, Steel, Jowett, Talbot, Parker, Krebs, Welch (Wearwell), Bezamet, Jacob (Belgium) and Faille (France). On the long, lonely stretches they had the flying 3 in sight. Although the speed rose to a crescendo, between Aberford and Wetherby 'Iron Man' Bedwell and Christison forced themselves from the bunch and up to the 12.

Still they hadn't caught the 3. Still they kept away, sneaking a glance back every now and again, but striving, ever striving to make certain that contact wasn't made. Johnny Pottier had missed the breaks and was back in the bunch to the tune of 2½ minutes, so the *maillot jaune* was to have a new owner.

As they came into the Stray at Harrogate, Tamburlini just sat up suddenly, and Mercier got his second stage, with Robbo taking second place and Tamburlini 3rd, 4 seconds back. The French pushed their lead in the Team race up to 3 minutes, and Tamburlini took the coveted yellow jersey.

Incredibly, at the end of the stage, the judges allowed the 3 leaders, 2 minutes and 25 seconds on the General Classification times, *as a bonus* for being delayed by the level-crossing. Perhaps this wasn't a hazard of the course!

STAGE 4. HARROGATE TO WHITLEY BAY 113 MILES.

It was raining hard as they waited for the flag to drop, and the Met men were no consolation in that the forecast was rain all day. Two of the Italians, Drei and Nascimbene, had packed it in and were already on their way back to Italy and sunshine. This left 47 in the field, and a very wet looking lot they were.

They were still in one big bunch at Ripon, but Tognaccini suddenly had his right-hand pedal unscrew on him and, what with this and the rain, he just turned it in! Just before Scotch Corner,

Guldemont of Belgium motored off, together with Pugi (Italy) and Robinson, but the field put their outboard motors out and soon pulled them back.

Guldemont went again. Again they pulled him back. Again he attacked, and off into the mire and mirk once more he went, this time taking with him Bedwell, Christison and Allamic (France). By Scotch Corner they had a meagre 40 seconds lead, and they had covered 37 miles in 1½ hours.

On to the Piercebridge road they hurried and Guldemont punctured; there he stood, rain dripping from all parts while he patiently waited for a wheel to be brought up. Sensation! Up the road a level-crossing was closed and Bedwell, Christison and Allamic were stopped. They jigged about in the rain for 45 seconds, the gates opened, the heavens opened, the field sighted them, and a real merry chase began.

They were really pounding it out when, just before West Auckland, Alf Newman (B.S.A.) hammered up to them, and hearts fluttered as they thought it was the main bunch. Up on Tow Law, tiny Bedwell went to town and took the *prime*.

Behind, Henry Guldemont had pulled out all the stops and had made it back to the bunch and was in the process of 'hedge-hopping' and passing through them. Came the feed at 75 miles and the gap gradually began to close. At Corbridge the front group was 17 strong, but at Houghton, 90 miles, the *peloton* was all together, except for Faille (France) who had gone hunting on his own.

It was on the outskirts of Newcastle that Bedwell, Christison, Krebs, Robinson, Tamburlini and Mercier caught him, and they hammered the daylights out of themselves, and breathed a real sigh of relief as the level-crossing gates at Earsdon opened just in front of them. They scrambled through, losing some seconds, and they slipped out of Earsdon with the bunch going berserk just a bare 100 yards behind.

On the narrow, twisted, winding roads to the coast they made time again, with Willi Jacob (Belgium) doing his nut between them and the *peloton*. He caught them with 1 mile to go, shattered it was true, but up there, but now it was Bedwell, Bedwell, all the way. He pulverised his opponents and won by 2 good lengths from Mercier, with Robinson at inches. And, not only did Bedwell win, but he got a bonus of 35 seconds as a slight compensation for the level-crossing delay. It never rains but it shines!

STAGE 5. WHITLEY BAY TO GLASGOW   158 MILES.

The rain held off for the start from outside the Rex Hotel, and the raincoated holiday crowds gave them a good send off. The 43 left in bade farewell to the sea and made inland northwards for the hills and dales of Scotland.

It was a biting nor'wester as they commenced the climb of Carter Bar. Ten miles of wet and windy misery lay before them, and Henri Guldemont had already left the fold, together with Johnny Welch. It was Johnny who took the *prime* prize, and then he sat up to wait for the rest of the field who were 1½ minutes back, but not so, Henri, for he pedalled on. It took another 10 miles before Mitchell and Newman caught him, but in a couple of miles they were absorbed by the bunch. The sun peeped out from behind rain-sodden clouds, and the French lads had 1 or 2 minor mishaps but soon got back on.

Rain fell again in sudden squalls as they made Walkerburn, and Maitland, Jackson (Ellis-Briggs), Faille, Fenwick and Faccioli (Italy) thought it a golden opportunity to get away. There were still 60 miles to go and the break was not regarded as being very serious. Maitland, who made the running was joined by Gaby Faille in about 3 miles, and then up came the rest. They worked hard, it was true, but the bunch were matching them, speed for speed.

Slowly, but relentlessly, the bunch began to gnaw at the distance between them. The 5 fugitives are slowing fast and only 5 miles to the finish, weary, dispirited, they were finally brought back. Freddy Krebs took his life in his hands, shot between two cars and was gone. Tamburlini saw the danger, whipped across the front of a mudguard but just could not make it – but Bezamat did. Les Wilson thundered up for the sprint, Parker hung on to his wheel like grim death.

Up went a marshal's hand. The leaders misunderstood and Wilson, Russell, Krebs, Jackson and Parker did a little dum-di-dum-di-dum along the road on their bottoms. Dennis Talbot (Hercules), always the one for a giggle, saw a tiny opening, went through it like a dose of Epsom and took the stage by lengths, although the judges said it was inches.

Behind him, Bezamat scrambled to 2nd place, with Maitland (at mere inches) 3rd. Tamburlini was still 1st and Mercier 2nd, on GC, and the French team could breathe easily again.

STAGE 6. GLASGOW TO MORECAMBE 167 MILES.

The weather relented at last and the sun shone. How lovely it was to stretch in some warmth, instead of cold dampness, for a change. The riders revelled in it, especially as their one and only 'rest' day had indeed been rough, weatherwise. Ian Steel had spent his day at home, but most of the other riders had spent the time in hotels many miles from Glasgow.

Don Wilson was out with trouble with his appendix, and Ken Mitchell (Wearwell) the 1953 Amateur Pursuit Champion was taking a real hammering in this, his first big stage race, and couldn't get much sleep. As he said 'I seem to be racing all day – and all night.'

Down at the People's Palace preparations were going on apace and 10.30 a.m. saw them on their way, on a route which was to take them across the Beattock Hills and Shap Fell.

Peter Pryor (B.S.A.) punctured 30 yards from the start, but within a mile was back. Henri Guldemont was stirring up the muck at the front, and breezed off on his own several times. As they climbed from Lesmahagow, off went Henri again, taking with him Stan Jones, Christison and Allamic and, out of the back came Den Talbot with a puncture, and it took Buttle and Joy, his team-mates to Beattock before they got him back to the bunch.

Up front, the merry four were winging their way through the feeding station, $1\frac{1}{2}$ minutes ahead of the *peloton*, and it was Ian Greenfield who went through like a bat out of hell, refusing food and drink, just to get up with the leaders. And how this man chases! Slowly he made ground, and at one point made up nearly 2 minutes in 6 miles, and had his just reward by catching the leaders just before the Border *Prime* at Gretna.

He went straight through, but Stan Jones was not having any and took the *prime* by a lick of paint, with Guldemont 3rd. They re-grouped and sped on their way with the main bunch at $2\frac{1}{2}$

minutes. Tentative moves were made as sorties from the bunch but they all came to naught.

As they hammered through Carlisle, lined with hundreds of people, with the lead held at 2½ minutes, the schedule of 23 m.p.h. was being maintained. At Penrith, they rode through a narrow funnel of people all cheering their heads off, and then they were out and on their way up Shap. The five commenced their battle with the giant, none gave an inch and it was Guldemont who made a sprint to end all sprints, to take the *prime* and become leader on the 'King of the Mountains'. Their lead was now 7 minutes!

From here it was virtually all downhill and how they made the most of it. Tyres sang merrily as they thrashed down through Kendal and Carnforth. Behind them, the *peloton* had been alerted, and pedals were being revved furiously, setting a new pace that was gradually pulling the leaders back. Mitchell and Faccioli forged ahead and attempted to get away from the bunch.

Along the Marine Road the five flew like homing pigeons, jockeying for position, safe in the knowledge that they could not be caught. First one, then another got the pole line, but it was Ian Greenfield who got his revenge on Stan Jones for the defeat at the Border by winning by 3 lengths, with Allamic at ½ a wheel, 3rd, Tamburlini was safe again.

STAGE 7.   MORECAMBE TO PRESTATYN   106 MILES.

There must have been a lot of hard thinking during the night, for the breakaway 5 of the previous day had made a name for themselves. Jones had jumped from 17th to 7th place; Allamic from 16th to 8th and Joe Christison had soared up to 5th place.

By the way the flags fluttered in the breeze, at least two-thirds of this stage was going to be with the wind behind. This was the stage in which Bedwell had lost 22 minutes the year before, and although not hard in the way of hills and terrain, was a stage that had to be treated with respect.

It was a brilliant, sunny Sunday, and there were thousands out in their cars, burning up petrol towards the coast. The *peloton* too was in a hurry and, as they sped through Lancaster, counter-attack followed attack. On through Preston and Wigan to War-

Eugene Tamburlini, the eventual winner of the 1954 Tour of Britain, climbing the Snake Pass on Stage 3

Leading the bunch during Stage seven of the 1954 Tour of Britain is E. Tamburlini of France, wearing the 'Yellow Jersey'

Bob Maitland (Hercules) leads out the riders from Islington Town Hall on the first stage of the 1955 Tour of Britain

THE TOUR OF BRITAIN - 1954

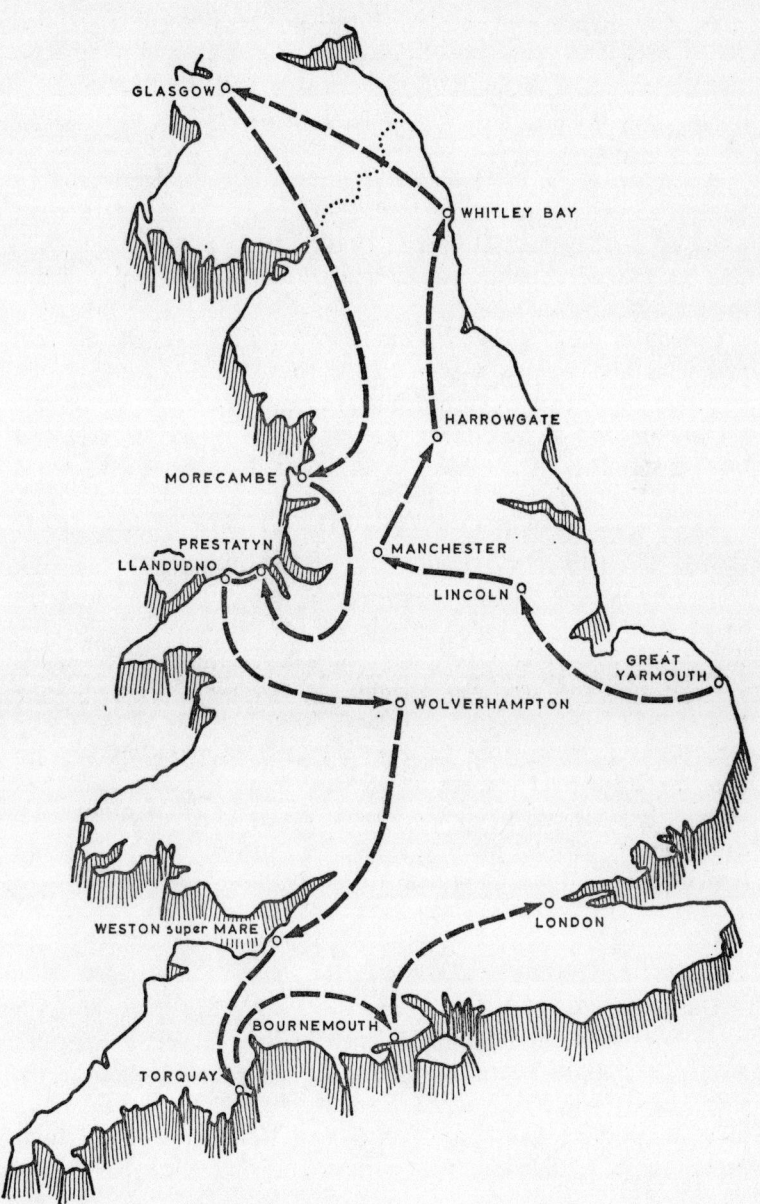

GLASGOW

WHITLEY BAY

HARROWGATE

MORECAMBE

PRESTATYN
LLANDUDNO

MANCHESTER

LINCOLN

GREAT YARMOUTH

WOLVERHAMPTON

WESTON super MARE

LONDON

BOURNEMOUTH

TORQUAY

rington and they had taken 2 hours for the 57 miles, and the tyres were really humming.

As they slipped over the Ship Canal Bridge, Faccioli (Italy) and Jacob (Belgium) went berserk and left the field, and were soon slightly ahead of Bedwell, Robinson, Joy and Tamburlini by ½ minute, and the rest, now beginning to split from here to Kingdom come at ¾ minute.

Along the A.56, everything was thrown into the battle and by Sutton Weaver there was a leading bunch of 22 riders. 5 more came up as they passed through Helsby, but 3 miles further on it was 'as you were', with only Germain Mercier, who had pulled a thigh muscle, behind.

Greenfield went away like an express train along the By-pass and with him went top time-trialist, Ken Joy. First into Wales was Ian, and then they turned into the teeth of the wind, with just a 1 minute lead. Behind them, the rest battled it out furiously, and out of the back went Alec Taylor, then Pottier, Welch, Wade (Gnutti-Cinelli), Jowett and Bev Wood.

There were no hills to contest, only the wind. Slowly, oh, so slowly, the pair made headway, inch by inch, yard by yard, second by hurting second. At Greenfield (pun?) they had 11 miles to go, and Ian then began to pile on the pressure. Life for Joy became no joy, as he was hammered left, right and centre. Came a slight rise and that was enough for Greenfield. He put in a tremendous burst that took him away from Ken Joy as though he had stopped. From here he just ploughed his way onwards to take the stage by 1 minute 55 seconds from Joy, who had been sighted, but not caught by the bunch. It was toughy Bedwell who came home 3rd, 1¼ minutes after Joy, and the 106 miles had been covered in 4 hrs. 6 mins. 25 seconds.

STAGE 8.　PRESTATYN TO LLANDUDNO　42 MILES.

This was time-trial day – *contre le montre,* the race of truth some say – and how revealing it was! In Britain, time-trialing has always had more adherents than road-racing and had, over the years, brought this side of the sport to a fine art. Here we had 42 miles of nothing like 'Boro' country, a virtual semi-circle from Prestatyn to Llandudno, with all sorts of hills, hair-pin bends, nerve-racking descents, even a humped-back bridge, plus a long exposed stretch along the coast into Llandudno.

An Italian, the only one left, was first to start, but he didn't appear. He was unwell! So, one by lonely one, with an interval of 2 minutes between them, they were sent on their way. Some of them were lucky and had Team Managers following in case of trouble. The others were not so lucky.

Peter Pryor, for instance, scooted his bike for the last 6 miles into Llandudno when his freewheel started freewheeling both ways. Bezamat, last man off, punctured where a stretch of road was under repair. Bob Maitland went slightly off course. Mercier toppled into a ditch when trying to pass a lorry in a narrow lane, was helped out by the lorry driver and sent on his way, only to go slightly off course 5 miles further on. Ken Russell managed to puncture twice.

But it was the stocky Bedwell who made the running, and it was Bedwell all the way over this tough, fiendishly devised course. With a time of 1.52.28 he seemed to have the stage sewn up, but he reckoned without the tail-end of the field.

Near the end came Guldemont, followed by Tamburlini, who in turn was followed by Brian Robinson. Guldemont caught Russell who had punctured, then Fenwick (Hercules) and was then caught by Eugene Tamburlini. And what a battle ensued now! They belted it out for mile after mile until Henri saw the 'black' and had had enough, and Eugene went on to record a fantastic 1.50.42 for the 42 breath-stopping miles and win the stage.

Germain Mercier had been in pain all night, and *only a pain-killing injection had enabled him to start at all.* Despite this, and the trouble he had en-route he still managed a very, very creditable time of 1.52.52 for 3rd place.

This fantastic ride had now put Tamburlini 5 minutes and 4 seconds ahead of his nearest rival Brian Robinson, and the French team had a real and secure hold over the Team race.

STAGE 9. LLANDUDNO TO WOLVERHAMPTON 116 MILES.

A light drizzle of rain plummeted out of heavy, overcast skies, and it was to be 116 miles of thrust and parry. They said 'goodbye' to the coast and within the first mile, Stan Jones and one or two others were already away.

Into the teeth of the wind they hustled and at Llanwrst it was Pryor and Pottier and Talbot who had 'bridged that gap' to haul back the first break. Welch squelched away at 28 miles and soon gained ½ minute.

From Corwen to Llangollen there were dry roads, and here we said 'ta-ta' to Ken Jowett (Viking) who had a damaged tendon muscle, which was to write 'finis' to his 1954 Tour. As they raced after Welch, it was Faille (France), Guldemont, and Doug Booker (Viking) who caught him, and after a further 7 miles up came Steel and Alf Newman to make a nice working group. Steel it was who took the Border *prime,* but Tarburlini smelt danger and brought up the bunch and all was one.

Christison attacked and at the feed had 20 seconds clear. Tamburlini missed his grub, but team-mate Plassa took 3, so they were all happy. Welch, Wilson and Des Robinson (Gnutti-Cinelli) skipped the wag, but after 8 miles were back looking sad and sorry, 'cos the wind was now really buffeting them on the side.

It was Henri Guldemont who took the initiative just before Harley Bank. Away he shot and with him for company went Joy, Des Robinson, Brian Robinson, Maitland, Mitchell, Parker and Scales. Bedwell did the proverbial hop, skip and jump and got between the two, and out came Joy and Parker, who helped their leader to get up there, only to find the redoubtable Henri Guldemont gone.

But wait! Lady Luck plays a fabulous part in stage-racing and it just wasn't the Belgian's day. He punctured at the foot of the hill. He changed, and within yards, the changed tyre went down. A spare wheel was given to him by a Service vehicle and it would not fit his machine, and there he was, near to tears and thoroughly dejected, waiting for his own team car at the side of the road.

Meanwhile, it is a sweating Les Scales who took the *prime* from Bedwell, but Scales dropped back, exhausted, while the tiny Bedwell raced on. Up came Newman, Brian Robinson, Mercier, Maitland and Pottier and at 106 miles, 3 more were added in Jacob (Belgium), Parker and Mitchell. With only 3 miles to go, another 4 were added in Russell, Corbusier (Belgium), Greenfield and Bezamat, but 'Bez' soon went off and crashed on the 'run-in' with Jackson (Ellis-Briggs).

Dave Bedwell made no mistake about it and went straight for the line, and only Ken Russell could get within a length of him, with Pottier at $2\frac{1}{2}$ lengths. This brought Bedwell up to 5th place on General Classification and only 1 point behind Henri Guldemont on the 'King of the Mountains'. Tamburlini was still 'sitting pretty' and the *maillot jaune* stayed on his shoulders for another day.

STAGE 10. WOLVERHAMPTON TO WESTON SUPER MARE 129 MILES.
The Frenchmen were in a commanding position, and they looked really confident as they lined up for the start from West Park. The thought that they would have to bash their heads against a head-wind all the way to Weston never seemed to bother them.

The ceremonial parade took longer than usual, and they were late in starting, but this was compensated for by cutting 4 miles out along the route, and the 133 advertised miles, became 129.

After an hour's hard riding in which they covered nearly $24\frac{1}{2}$ miles, there were 17 away to but a slight lead. Doug Booker was there, and scarpered away on his own, picking his way daintily through the heavy traffic of Worcester. He was left out there, battling it out for some 17 miles before being hauled back by Welch, Newman, Jomaux and Guldemont, they had a lead of $1\frac{3}{4}$ minutes, but this was cut to 50 seconds at Tewskesbury.

At Twigworth, the pattern had changed again, and then came the climb up to Stroud and Nailsworth, and it was Guldemont, without effort, who took the *prime*. Welch blew his bellows and went out the back. Ken Mitchell punctured in the *peloton* but soon managed to get back, while Jomaux had crashed, but rode like a maniac to get back on.

15 formed up to make a new lead group, but each and every one was being watched closely. Bedwell punctured, and was back in the fold even as the last man passed. After the feeding station, Willi Jacob (Belgium) ploughed a lonely furrow out front for 20 odd miles, including the long run down to Bath and over the switchbacks of the Mendip Hills.

One or two had a go to get with Jacob, but all got hauled

back. There was no purposeful racing, but the speed was there and could not be denied. Maitland went. So did Steel, but were prevented from getting too far by Tamburlini. 7 miles to go and it was Mercier who broke clear, but it was Ken Joy, together with team-mates Parker and Bedwell, who snatched him back. Corbusier took a dive and ate dirt as his forks suddenly disintegrated under him.

On to the fenced-off seafront the 38 riders rocketed, and it was an elbows-out, knees bent, head-wagging thrust towards the finish, but there was never any doubt when Bedwell rocketed out of the screaming pack to take a 2 length lead and hold off Les Wilson (B.S.A.) with team-mate Parker at a further length.

It had been negative racing, but it now brought Dave Bedwell up to 4th place on General Classification.

STAGE 11. WESTON SUPER MARE TO TORQUAY 91 MILES.

There they were, the 39 couriers left in, outside the Winter Gardens Pavilion, oblivious to the rumble of talk of the spectators, press men, or the rattle of the news-reel cameras. They listened to Team Managers telling them of the hazards and tactics for the day.

All too soon they were away and for the first 28 miles it was a time-trialist's dream, but then came the nightmare of the climbs up, over, down and round the Great Haldon hills, before the finish in Torbay Road, Torquay.

8 miles out of Weston, on a long, straight road reaching out seemingly to nowhere, Bedwell flashed away, with Fenwick, Taylor, Booker, Guldemont, Maitland, Jones, Failles and others. Along the broad expanse of the A.38 the battle was fought out at 30 m.p.h. plus and it was Plassa who finally made contact and brought them back.

Again the Hercules riders went, throwing everything into short bursts of speed that thrill the onlooker and chill the marrow off the bones of the other contestants. This time it is Talbot and with him goes Ian Greenfield, and at Taunton they had a lead of $2\frac{1}{2}$ minutes. They were to stay clear all day, for the French hung on grimly, not letting anyone else go, and chasing anything that moved. At 40 miles, the tandem was $4\frac{3}{4}$ minutes clear and they held this for many miles. Greenfield had won the Marsh Hill *prime* for Talbot had not bothered to contest it.

At Crewkerne, the lead was down to four minutes, and suddenly Steel and Scales threw everything in except the kitchen sink and got away from the 'froggies' notice. It was no holds barred and 8 fantastic miles later they were but 2 minutes behind the leaders and 2 minutes in front of the bunch. Along the Exeter By-pass they thundered and right near the end had the two fugitives in sight. Steel rode like a maniac but the speed was too much for Scales and he was left floundering in Steel's wake as he belted on, alone. On the tough Telegraph Hill Steel got within 20 seconds of the tandem but never quite made it. The field had woken up and were 3½ minutes back.

Then battle really commenced. The lead in time see-sawed back and forth with Steel getting up towards the leaders, then falling back and Scales nearly catching him. Into the run-in they scrambled and Talbot and Greenfield sprinted for the line, with Ian getting the verdict by a length, with Ian Steel, 46 seconds behind, 3rd, and Scales 4th, a further 15 seconds back.

Steel, Greenfield and Talbot went up on General Classification, but the Wearwell team have hopped over the Hercs, and were now in 2nd place, just over 4 minutes down on the French, and just over 1 minute clear of the Hercules men. With 2 days still to go, anything might have happened to the Team Race for 4 minutes was nothing at that stage.

STAGE 12.   TORQUAY TO BOURNEMOUTH   115 MILES.

Again the rains came. Skies were a dirty grey, and a wet, cold drizzling rain fell as they lined up for the 'off' at Beacon Quay. There were only 2 stages left now, and it was on this one that anyone who wanted to make a name for himself must make the effort.

And what a start it was! No sooner was the neutralised period over than they are already at it. It was Bob Maitland who thrashed away to open up the first gap, but got pulled back for his trouble. He went again at Dawlish and, on a fiercesome climb hammered the field all the way to the top, and the first hour went by with 25 miles covered.

95

Tamburlini, red-nosed and sniffing, because he was nursing an almighty cold, attacked along the Exeter By-pass, and it was the stocky Bedwell who sat on him. On through Honiton, and one after another, they all had a go, but no one succeeded. Up to the *prime* just outside Yarcombe and Freddy Krebs punctured. Buttle just stopped and gave him his bike and he was back in the bunch before you knew that he had been off.

The top of the hill was shrouded in mist and it was Brian Robinson who took it from Alec Taylor and Tamburlini. Henri Guldemont was content to sit in for the 'King of the Mountains' title was already his.

The pace got hotter as they belted through Chard and they passed through Crewkerne, and that's 62½ miles in 2½ hours. The break finally came when you least expected it, and it was *contre le montre* man Ken Joy who engineered it, helped by Alec Taylor, Tamburlini, Maitland, Ilsley, Brian Robinson and others in very, very close attendance. 15 men it was got that way, and only one of them was from the Wearwell team. Someone had rocked the boat and they had missed the vital break.

In the chasing *peloton,* the Wearwell team were going crazy. They put everything they had left into the kitty for this one, just to get a couple more men up there with the leaders. They tried, tried again and failed. They tried yet again, pushing the speed up to heights from which riders went off smashed, and completely finished, and finally, exhausted spent the last 50 miles chasing a myth that was but 1 minute away.

At 7 miles to go, Clive Parker thought it was 3, and forged ahead. When he found out his mistake, he shrugged his shoulders and just kept going, and so full of punch were his last few miles that he took the stage from Bezamat (France) by 31 seconds, with Bob Maitland, 3rd at inches.

I said previously, anything might happen and it had for Wearwell dropped back to 3rd place on Team Classification, and now there was only one day to go!

STAGE 13. BOURNEMOUTH TO LONDON 120½ MILES.

The question being asked by the French was, 'Would it be a *promenade* to the finish?' They were satisfied in their own minds

The lead group on the climb of the Brecons during the 1955 Circuit of Britain

Viv Bailes, the 1954 Circuit winner, is greeted by Eileen Sheridan, women's record holder at the finish of the 1954 Circuit of Britain

Raymond Holliday (23) of Wolverhampton and Royal Air Force Cycling Association passing the line to win the garland for the third day of the 1955 Amateur Circuit of Britain Cycle Race

that they had won, but the British lads made no bones about the fact that this was a fight to the death, even although they were but fighting it out for second place, and battle between the Hercules and Wearwell teams would continue right up to the finish line.

It was a glorious day – the best of the Tour. The sun shone warmly, and although the French considered that it was all over, there were those who calculated that if Brian Robinson could get a lead of 2½ minutes and with the 2 minutes bonus for the stage win . . . still, there are always the suppositionists!

Out from the Pavilion Forecourt pour the 39 riders left in. Out on to the main A.39 highway, crowded with spectators at all the vantage points. The motorbikes roared, the tyres hummed in the peace of the day, but there was no peace within the *peloton*.

It surged and swayed. It bulged and blended back into a mass. It was a maelstrom of activity that never ceased. There were attacks which never really got started. There were heartaches in galore. The vortex sped on and on, the middle out to the sides and then back in again. At Ower, Stan Jones took life and limb in hand, made a fantastic sprint and there was a gap. Soon he was a minute in the lead and going like a bomb. His lead never reached any more than 1 minute 5 seconds, and on the A.30 they hammered him into the dust near Sutton Scotney, and that was that.

Came a lull and, at the Green Man, Maitland went and with him, from the other side of the pack went Guldemont. You could see the hurt and agony in their faces as they put everything into this one desperate burst to be the first to the line on this day. They worked themselves into a frenzy, eyes glazed and staring ahead in this all-out effort. Behind them, tiny Bedwell had gone berserk and was thrashing his way through the bunch, out, and into the chase of the flying two.

The tiny figure put every ounce of remaining strength into getting up there with Henri and Bob, and it was the thrill of a lifetime to thousands packed into the Alexandra Palace when 'Iron Man' Bedwell caught Maitland but 200 yards from the finishing line and with one last desperate and despairing plunge he got past Guldemont only yards from the line, on that hard last climb. So exhausted was he that he couldn't even lift his head and acknowledge the cheers. Meanwhile, Bezamat had stormed up and, in the last few yards had taken 3rd place from Maitland.

And so the Tamburlini 'Tour' was over. Congratulations were showered on everyone at the banquet, and officials and competitors were praised for their high standard of conduct, and there were hopes that all the foreign teams would be back in the following year, but this was the death knell of the 'Tour of Britain' by the *Express*.

6: The 'Holiday Camp Tour'

Tour of Britain, 1955
September 3rd—10th

Everyone knew that, unless the rival bodies could get together in harmony before the 1955 season. the *Express* would cease to sponsor the event. A nation-wide newspaper strike didn't help matters and, as it was blatantly apparent that an agreement between the League and the Union was nowhere in sight, they dropped the 'Tour'.

The National Cyclists Union, who had, at one time, over 80,000 members, were getting the 'stick', and were facing a rapidly dwindling membership. They stepped into the breach and assured their members that *they* were going to put on a 'Tour of Britain'. They based all their hopes on backing from the cycle trade, which was very dicey at that time, because a lot of changes were going on within the industry. They had no-one who could, with authority, say that they could run a 'Tour' and were eventually forced to abandon the whole idea, which did a great deal of harm and won many converts to the League.

The League, through Doug Peakall, stepped in, and Doug was given the job of putting on the 1955 'Tour of Britain', and he did it, in just six weeks! During those weeks, Doug worked like a trojan and really went to town, and the list of sponsors that he obtained reads like the pages of a Cycling Debrett. There was Bayliss-Wiley; British Hub Co.; Brooks Saddles; B.S.A. Cycles; Butlins Holiday Camps; Cyclo Gears; S. J. Clark; Dunlop Rubber Co.; Fibrax Ltd.; G.B. Components; Gills Cables; Hercules Cycles; Viking Cycles, etc., etc.

That great sportsman, Billy Butlin weighed in with accommodation at some of his holiday camps, and a giant trophy, while the other sponsors made it possible to present over £1,000 in prizes. Donations poured in from small firms, and it is these nameless 'wonders' who turned the tide and made the whole thing possible.

Such was the state of the sport at that time that the Independent class (riders who couldn't make up their minds whether to be Amateurs or Professionals) had to be 'bolstered' up and although two 'foreign' teams in Belgium and an 'International' team, consisting of riders from Switzerland, Italy, Monaco and Belgium were down to compete, there were still too few competitors and a new class of rider, known as 'Aspirants', was thought up to give the event volume, at least at the start.

These 'Aspirants' were Amateurs signed up for the 'Tour' supposedly to give some sign of activity to the League 'Tour de France' plan, which was nothing more than a thought and never came to fruition. However, there were ten 'bods' who were keen enough to have a go and made up two teams, Sheffield City and London. Nobody gave them a lot of thought, because the Hercules team had been on the continent all the season, and had been doing very nicely, thank you.

The League too, had dipped heavily into their own resources, and by the end of the 'Tour' had a substantial amount of money to find to pay out, but such was the spirit within the League itself that there was no question of how the money would be found . . . it just would be found.

STAGE 1. LONDON (BIGNALLS CORNER) TO CLACTON 74 MILES.

Never one to do things by halves, Doug Peakall arranged for the race to assemble outside Islington Town Hall on a Saturday morning, and heaven help the coster-mongers from the Chapel Street Market!

A high wind swept up the debris of the dance the night before, and traffic got past somehow with the help of a lot of bantering good humour. Riders had been 'briefed' the night before at Reggiori's Restaurant in Kings Cross, and quite a number of them were none the wiser for it! Doug saw to it that he had the 'only bit of paper' in existence, and while there wasn't much chance of the Union nobbling the race, he personally, wasn't taking any chances.

There had been an objection to 10 men from the Hercules 'equipe' starting and this had been cut back to five. There were one or two odd looking jerseys floating around, as though someone hadn't quite made up their minds as to what this or that particular rider's jersey was to look like, but they were all neat and tidy and, with so little funds in hand to do anything with, who cared anyway?

For such short notice there was a vast crowd as the riders lined up, and the Mayor, after a speech of welcome, sent them on their way, led out by June Thackeray, the B.L.R.C. Ladies Champion. Traffic was heavy up the North Road to Bignalls Corner, and there they all dismounted and had lunch.

The sun was ready for roasting as, at 2 p.m. they set off along the Barnet By-pass, and Jean Borcy (Belgium) was out front, whipping 'em up. In 2 miles, Tony Hewson and Dick Bartrop, new Aspirants from Sheffield are clear and, as they run into the lanes, the elastic twangs, and they were back in the bunch. Such was the beating being handed out that every yard you got clear had to be earned the hard way – by working.

The narrow, winding roads to Hertford are full of market traffic, and along here a bunch of 13 sneaked off, but traffic lights brought them to a halt. Came another 13 miles of lanes to Bishops Stortford, and Pottier (Wearwell), Christison (Viking), Syd Wilson (Russell/Wilson) and 10 more got clear, and were being chased by Scales and Guldemont at 45 seconds, and Ian Steel, Moxhet (Belgium) and Jock Andrews (London) leading the bunch.

Before they reached the A.12 near Colchester, the bunch began to move up and the fugitives were absorbed, but Wren (Sheffield) punctured and did not make it back, and Hinch (Russell/Wilson) suffered the same fate in Braintree. Two down and the rest belted on.

Maitland (Hercules) and Hewson tried a long one along the Colchester By-pass, but the field would not have it, and it was left until the last 15 miles before the decisive move was made. Joe Christison suddenly wound it up, and behind him, fluttering in the stiff wind went Penvose (Leaguer); Talbot (Hercules); Syd Wilson and Van Dorpe (International), with Johnny Morris (London) waggling in the breeze.

This was it! As the race swung off on to the 'B' class road

these six were out of sight, and everyone was suddenly hammering everyone else. It was chaos in so narrow a road, and those who wanted to get to the front and have a go at the leaders were baulked, and those at the front did not seem to be able to get going fast enough.

But the whole was disconcerting enough for the flying six to get the bit between their teeth and get that few vital seconds 'edge' on the field, and even they were belting the daylights out of one another. Joe Christison started another wind-up and they hurtled towards the gates of Butlins, and it was Syd Wilson and Van Dorpe slightly in the lead, and sprinting *past the gate!*

The mistake was rectified after a few highly skidded yards but, by this time, little Joe had beaten Penvose by $\frac{1}{2}$ length, with Talbot at 15 seconds; Van Dorpe at 16 seconds; Wilson at 20, and a wilting Morris at 23 seconds, with the rest of the field at 58 seconds. Christison (Viking) took the first yellow jersey, and Viking took the team award as well.

STAGE 2.   CLACTON TO SKEGNESS   152 MILES.

The water in the pool looked inviting, even at 10 a.m. as they started out from the camp, but they were out of the gate with Christison still tugging his *maillot jaune* into place. Talbot stopped with loose handlebars, but got back, and four miles from Colchester, Mattivi (Italy) and Fourneau (Belgium) locked handle bars and looked lovingly in one another's eyes.

Mattivi was in trouble again at Colchester and, although Moxhet waited for him, he did not seem to be in any hurry. At Sudbury, 3 riders shot off, and Steel, Ilsley (Hercules) and Guldemont made a nice lead of $3\frac{1}{4}$ minutes by the time Long Melford rolled beneath their wheels, and somehow, Dick Bartrop had got up there.

Behind them, the field suddenly woke up, got off their bottoms and, soon there was a chasing group of Pottier, Stratford (Leaguer); Jowett (Viking); Doug Petty (Russell/Wilson) and N.C.U. Champion, Graham Vines (Wearwell) who were going at it, hammer and tongs, and they soon caught Jock Andrews who had escaped on his own. What effort they put into the chase could be imagined by the fact that by 50 miles they had caught the leaders, and it was Henri Guldemont who was whipping them up to a frenzy.

Behind them, there was a lot of hot and harassed faces. At the feeding station at Stratford the lead was 3 minutes, and at Wareham, Petty died the death. Up to Outwell, 13 miles further on, and you could hear Guldemont shouting 'Alez, Alez, Alez' as they came past, and it certainly was 'Alez', because the first of the bunch came through 6¼ minutes later.

The wind was flattening the grasses across the Fens, and they echeloned out while Henri went from the back in an almighty effort, and they were content to let him stay out there and rot. Vines has a wash from his bottle (what – no soap and towel?) and with 15 miles to go, 9 were still together. Guldemont content now to be back in the fold gives Steel a drink from his bottle, and they settled down for the run-in.

They snaked into Skegness and made for the camp; so chill was the day that there were not many out to cheer them on their way. Vines mistook a right-hander and Dick Bartrop screamed through to take the stage by one lonely second from Vines, with Jock Andrews at inches, and the other 6 breathing down the back of their necks.

STAGE 3. SKEGNESS TO FILEY 110 MILES.

Such had been the rush to get the 'Tour' under way, that the mileages had never been properly checked and were never the same as those printed in the programme. Bartrop put on his yellow jumper and the 45 riders started into the wind for the 73 miles road-race jaunt, and within a mile there was torrential rain.

Mitchell (Wearwell) broke clear and scudded up the road, followed by Steel, Andrews, Vermaelen (Belgium) and Fourneau. By Burgh-le-Marsh the whole had split into three groups, each one suffering as badly as the next, and Blissett (London) had bid a soggy farewell. Through blinding rain they pounded on and Short (Sheffield) suddenly got short of breath and dropped back to join Blissett.

Right up at the front the leaders were forging ahead, and the spray bounced back at them from the road; behind them echelon after echelon was being formed like so much dirty washing. On the undulating road to Louth, daylight began to show between wheels, and the end was nigh. Bartrop was up at the front of the chasers slamming 'em round, but at Market Rasen the hurrying 5 have a lead of 3½ minutes. Outside Caistor a level-crossing gate was closed and by the time they got going the lead had been whittled down.

Climbing out of Caistor, Mitchell and Andrews drew away, and although Steel and Forneau chased it was only the Belgian who made it, while Steel had to be content to form up with Vermaelen. Up, down and round the hair-pins at Brigg they went and then on to Hull. The leading 3 made minutes on the tandem, with the bunch rapidly losing interest. And wonder of wonders, it had stopped raining.

The two English lads attacked, but the Belgian made it back, counter-attacking to make the two work. They pulled him back, and he attacked again. Back he came and suddenly they were running in to the finish. The 200 yard flag stood out against the grey sky. Forneau looked up, saw the flag and hammered the daylights out of himself to get there. He made it, but the finishing flag was a further 200 yards up the road, and it was Jock Andrews (London) who made it by 2 lengths from Mitchell (Wearwell) with Forneau (Belgium) ½ length away 3rd. The Belgians protested, long, loudly and vociferously but they fell on thick ears.

There was some fun and games at the Ferry, because someone had to wait for Johnny Short. Away went the boat and there was organiser Doug Peakall dancing a fandango on the quay, having been left behind while he'd been getting the tickets. All ended well, lunch was partaken, and then came the *contre le montre,* and it was Viking's Joe Christison who performed 1.28.25 for first place, followed by Dick Bartrop (Sheffield) 1.29.03, and third, Vincenti Mattivi (Italy) with 1.30.08. Bartrop retained the *maillot jaune* and Viking the team.

STAGE 4.   FILEY TO SHEFFIELD   95 MILES.

The day was hot and humid as they left the coast behind and hammered inland. 8 miles went by and Vines, followed by Forneau, Ilsley, Andrews, Mitchell and Bartrop led the bunch.

Staxton and Driffield came and went, and Russenberger (Switzerland) was in trouble with his back wheel, and Syd Wilson got tailed off. Guldemont was chasing the field like mad having had wheel trouble and Jean Borcy and Vermaelen were with him. By Bainton, all the lost souls were back in the fold, hot, bothered, but looking none the worse for wear.

It was like a game of chess really, as first one rider, then another, went off the front, was brought back, and made up a different pattern. Some sat up and drank, others chewed a banana, or just the fat.

One by struggling one they breezed off and, forming up, were soon chasing each other like mad and soon there were 14 in Bartrop, Waterfield and Hewson (Sheffield), Robinson, Gill and Christison (Viking), Mitchell and Pottier (Wearwell), Hoar (Hercules), Morris (London), Borcy, Guldemont, Ernest Albert and Van Dorpe (Belgium). They were in a deuce of a hurry and soon put 5 minutes between themselves and the chasers.

Over Boothferry Bridge and on to Pontefract, the pattern was the same. You do your job and I'll do mine seemed to be the order of the day, and behind them, General Classification was being spread far and wide. Maitland and Vines collected a couple of tintacks but got back. The *peloton* stirred itself out of its lethargy, stretched, but it was only the death-throes.

More moves were being made up front. Christison punctured in Hemsworth, and the lads missed a fine chance to leave him behind, for Bobby Thom ordered him to take Gill's bike, and he was back on within a mile. As they belted along the By-pass, three up bottoms and take off, with a fourth chasing and they soon are nearly out of sight. Traffic lights nearly halted the chasers and they lost 15 seconds.

There were five miles to go, and Waterfield turned green and couldn't take any more, having lead in his legs and sickness in his stomach. He tried to get back on on a stiffish hill, but it was pitiful even to watch and he sank back into oblivion.

With only 1½ miles to go, Christison and Mitchell sprung to life and along the Barnsley By-pass they made road, and Borcy somehow, got up there with them. At a mile to go, they were still away, and were still at it, hammering it out, yard by hammering yard. Coming up to the 200 yard mark, it was Tony Hoar who took off, passing Mitchell who had blown up completely, then Borcy, and then Des Robinson and, on the final drag up to the finish, he crossed the line 4 lengths ahead of Robinson.

STAGE 5. SHEFFIELD TO PWLLHELI   168 MILES.

This day ended but 1 mile short of the longest stage ever, and a hot sun oppressed the riders, as they left the 'flat' behind for the mountains of the Peak District and Wales. Russenberger was on his way home with tummy trouble.

On the long climb out of Sheffield they had time to take stock, but as they dropped down the other side, the colourful cavalcade had already begun to look a little pock-marked. Vines, unable to sleep (a well-known 'Tour' hazard) was already off the back and struggling, while Brian Haskell was sitting perkily at the front.

From the 'hair-pin' on Mam Tor we saw a speck appear, check watch, and it was a minute before 3 more appeared, and then the bunch. Slowly he came into visual range, and it was Haskell, climbing like a monkey, and 45 seconds behind him came Forneau and Gill, with 2 minutes covering the field. Haskell did not wait and on he tore, up, down, round, back and 10 miles further on took the second *prime* from Guldemont and Russell. Vines had retired.

Trouble there was a'plenty, as Hoar snapped a pedal spindle, and Waterfield broke a rear spindle, and lost 15 minutes 'cos his team car broke down on Mam Tor! Wren and Short were trailing, and it was a long, long trail.

At Middlewich, there was a lead group of 27 riders, and the speed was barely 20 m.p.h. After a long and lonely chase, Hoar had got back on. 2 more miles went by and away went Steel, Andrews, Russell, Penvose and Talbot to make a break that nearly came to naught as the level-crossing at Nantwich was closed. Up and over the steps they raced and, at the feed, led by 1¾ minutes. Auquier (Belgium) had punctured and retired. Moxhet (Belgium) had gone off course.

The *peloton* began to move up and between Whitchurch and Ruabon made contact. Came the beautiful vale of Llangollen and, with 70 miles to go Booker (Viking) got away, and Mattivi and Albert (Belgium) caught him. He stopped working, but they went on, and after 15 hectic miles in which Booker did absolutely

THE TOUR OF BRITAIN - 1955

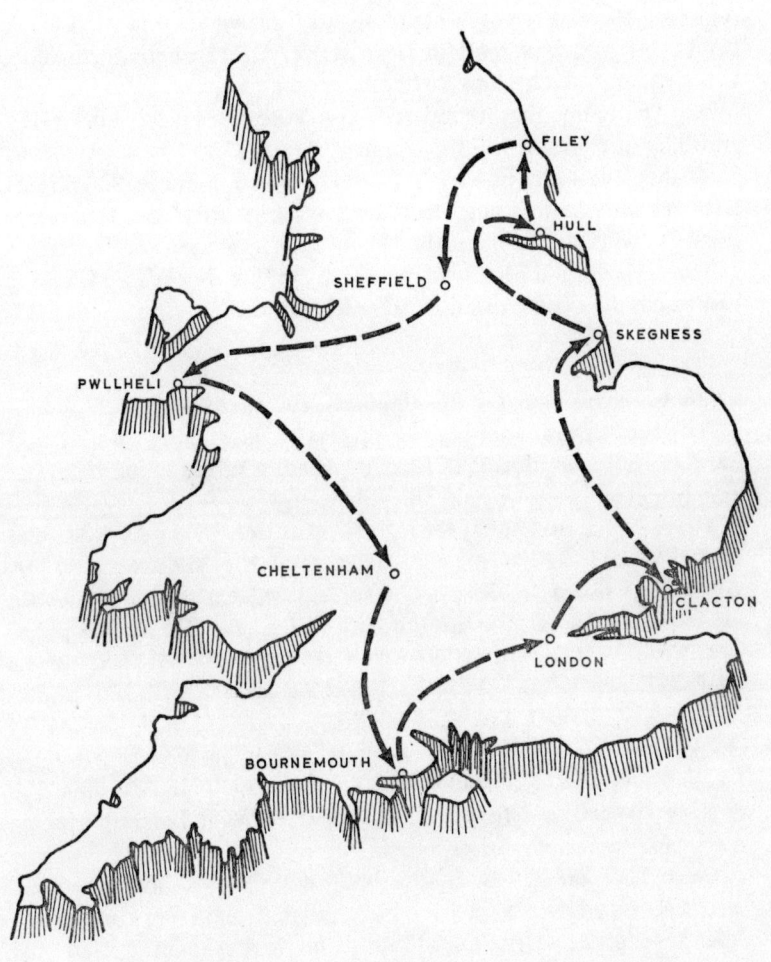

nothing, Mattivi jumped suddenly and went it alone. Behind him there came Steel, Russell, Andrews, Haskell, Ian Brown (Wearwell), Hewson and Pusey (Hercules) chasing, and in 20 miles, the *peloton*, who had obviously stopped for a nap, were 11 minutes down.

They caught Albert and, at Conway Falls, with 40 miles to go, he and Haskell punctured and never made it back. At Blaenau-Ffestiniog there was a fantastic battle for the *prime*, and it was Aspirant Hewson who showed the way. Down they hurtled, took bends, bridges, and road in their stride. On through Portmadoc, Criccieth and, finally into Pwllheli.

Into the camp they thundered, and Pusey disgraced himself by grabbing the saddle of the winning Mattivi, and was penalised. Steel was 2nd with Booker 3rd, and it was 7 minutes 22 seconds later when Mitchell, who had done a 'solo' from the last *prime* came in, with the field nearly $11\frac{1}{2}$ minutes down on the leaders.

Tony Hewson it was who took the 'yellow duster', and Viking had nearly 20 minutes on the International team.

STAGE 6. PWLLHELI TO CHELTENHAM   162 MILES.

Another testing, soul-searing day, with long, long climbs, and even longer runs down. A side or head wind most of the way, and bright hot sun to help the riders on their way.

They hammered out through Portmadoc, Trawsfynydd and Dolgelley and, in less than 20 miles came the Maentwrog *prime*, which was taken by Mitchell who climbed this tough mountain effortlessly, after team-mate Pottier had led out. The second *prime* saw Forneau take on all and sundry and beat Mitchell to the 'cleft in the rocks'.

Talbot, Gill and Des Robinson attacked and were joined by Booker and, as we swept in through the rolling hills and through Llanerfyl they had a lead of 45 seconds. At 75 miles came the feeding station, and they were all together, with Bartrop winning the sprint for the Border *prime*.

From here on it was Guldemont's day. He just looked round, sprinted, sat down, looked round, sprinted and swept away and just kept going. By Church Stoke he had a minute lead and gradually, by dint of really hard work, built this up, second by second, minute by minute, while behind him the field dangled in space, seemingly unworried and in a vacuum. Within 5 miles he was 3 minutes ahead, and there was *still over 70 miles to go*.

He settled down to his mighty task. He the hare, being chased, perhaps reluctantly, by the hounds. A measured rhythm seemed to come into his legs and they commenced to turn the pedals evenly up hill and down dale. For mile after lonely mile he ploughed a lonely furrow, through Craven Arms, Ludlow and on to the second feeding station with 47 miles to go, and he now had *8 minutes* in hand on the *peloton*.

They had begun to realise, at last, that this man was dangerous, and the bunch just went berserk. Not one, or a couple, or a small group of chasers. Oh no! It became a *mass* pursuit. Up and up and up went the speed as they madly hurtled down the road after this fool who had been out there so long. Down, down, down came Guldemont's lead as 40, 50 and 60 lonely, lonely miles were registered. You could see now the utter weariness in the man's face and he had his bad moments, but he never faltered.

The lead tumbled down, and down tumbled the miles. He was fighting hard now, with the wind more than a little troublesome. Came a long, straight stretch of road and the thirsty chasers saw him for the first time. The *peloton* was descending like a pack of maniacs, while Guldemont was climbing. He pounded on, putting everything into this last superb effort. 3 miles to go, 2 miles, 1½ miles to the finish and *still* they had not made contact.

He was out of the saddle now, weary, oh so weary, and there was just one mile to go. Round a double bend, through a couple of Halt signs, that he could not have possibly seen and cost him ten bob in fines, and finally he shambled into the Albert Road. It must have felt like, and looked like, miles to the finishing line as he ambled his triumphant way to the line. There was no huge crowd to cheer him in, just a handful of people and officials, but they, small in number as they were, raised the roof for this truly fantastic ride. It was 28 seconds later that the bunch thundered across the line led in by Tony Hoar and with Hercules team-mate Pusey, 3rd.

STAGE 7. CHELTENHAM TO BOURNEMOUTH 104 MILES.

It seemed as though 1 minute they were in Cheltenham, and the next, many miles away, so fast did they motor. At 16 miles they were all together, and the 34 men left in were really pounding it out.

Came the first *prime* at Blunsdon, and it was Forneau (Belgium) making sure of the 'King of the Mountains' from Haskell. Off shot Christison, followed at short intervals by Hoar and Scales. By 54 miles. Scales had managed to stay with Christison, but would not work, and Hoar was all of a minute behind. On Marlborough Hill, so much did they muck about, Hoar caught them and went on up to take the *prime*, and then linked up with Christison, which made Scales an 'also ran'.

Through a cloudburst on Salisbury Plain they hurried, with thunder, lightning, and unearthly fireworks banging away and lighting up the scene, as heavy rain lashed down. Hoar had to change a damaged wheel and Joe Christison ambled on alone. We now had one man, being chased by one, who was being chased by Scales, who was being chased by the field.

At Shipton Bellinger we shot out on to bone-dry roads, and the three are together again, just over one minute in the lead of the *peloton*. Scales was the 'shop steward' and was urging them on, and Christison was telling him what to do with himself. The bunch was lackadaisical and at this point should have pulled them back. Hoar was just sitting there letting the other two argue it out.

Forneau broke clear and left the bunch to its own devices, and belted out for all points south and, with only 11 miles to go up he came like a bolt from the blue, and the 3 had now become 4. He whipped them up into a frenzy which did not really get any more speed out of them, and then just as suddenly quietened down and sat in to wait for the finish.

Into King's Park and it was no holds barred. They threw everything, race wise, at one another, and it was a deadly battle right up to the line, with Forneau really blotting his copy book by pulling Les Scales' saddle and getting relegated by penalisation to 4th place. So it was Scales 1st, Hoar 2nd and Joe Christison 3rd. There were no protests from the Belgians, and the 30 strong bunch came in 35 seconds later, having been slightly delayed by traffic lights on the run in.

Hewson, Aspirant extraordinary, was in there with them and now led by 1 minute 13 seconds, from Ken Mitchell, with Dick Bartrop at 3 minutes 27 seconds. Viking had a firm hold on the team race.

STAGE 8. BOURNEMOUTH TO LONDON (HAMPSTEAD HEATH) 118 MILES.
This was the finale, the be all to end all! The battle was still on, and would be, right up to the last climb up that hill to the White Stone Pond at Hampstead. It was to be a terrific mental strain for many of the riders. Hewson and Bartrop, new men at the 'Tour' game, had to keep away from Mitchell, Christison and Guldemont. The Wearwell team had to keep alert to keep away from the International and Hercules 'equipes', and so the last stage was set, not for the usual 'promenade', but a 'race' from the word 'go'.

Through the New Forest and Talbot left the bunch to fend for itself. He was riding like a maniac and Haskell was throwing everything into a frenzy of movement to get up with him. A tanker got in the way, and the two made hay and soon had a two minute lead.

On through Romsey they hammered and on to Kings Somborne and on the climb out, Talbot gave a glance backwards and nearly stopped dead in his tracks, for coming up fast, but fast, were Booker, Blissett and Wren. At 41 miles these 5 were together and had a 2 minute 20 second lead.

So 5 sweating lads worked themselves to a bonanza, honking up the hills, hurtling down the other side, bit-and-bitting, with a slight tail-wind helping them along. As they passed through Blackwater with 40 miles to go they had a clear lead on 10 minutes, and the bunch certainly did not seem to be too worried. After all Hewson had a 17 minute lead on Booker!

It was fortunate really that Wearwell could see their second place in the team race slipping away and so they began to move up, and so gradually eased the problem. In the bunch, Forneau was breaking every rule in the book, riding through traffic lights, taking food from a travelling vehicle, and just being a ruddy, childish, fool. Over the Chertsey Bridge they trundled and Forneau took a drink, sat up, poured the rest over his head, and just dropped out of the back.

111

Mitchell was giving Hewson a hammering, throwing in short, sharp bursts of speed that had Tony hanging on by his rudder and every slight rise, roundabout and parked car is used to pry him from his slender lead. He took it all and came back for more, and slowly they got nearer and nearer to the finishing point.

Meanwhile, up front, the 5 jolly little escapees were doing their nuts, and they screamed round the lights into Hendon Way and then left and commenced the steep climb up to the finish. It was Doug Booker who finally slipped the leash, rounding off his Tour with a last stage win by 4 seconds from Talbot, with Brian Haskell at 15 seconds, and the other two, on their knees – Blissett at 26 seconds and Wren at 34 seconds.

The field belted in 8 minutes and 11 seconds later, including Hewson, Mitchell and Bartrop, and the 1955 'Tour of Britain' was over, with the professionals well and truly humbled.

The little Italian Restaurant in Theobalds Road (gone now), chosen for the after-race dinner, resounded with chatter. The top table was devoid of anyone except the League Chairman, Eddie Lawton and his wife Audrey. Race officials had taken exception (once again) to anyone but themselves being on the top table, even although most of us were paying around 12/6 each for our meal.

In the speeches, the dripping platitudes were there, the backslapping and the bonhomie, with the underlying current of tension. The prizewinners received their acclaim, Forneau, now with his good humour recovered, for his win in the 'King of the Mountains', the Viking team for taking the team race, but it was Aspirant, Tony Hewson who received the real acclamations, and the Butlin Trophy from Audrey Lawton, and undoubtedly it was Tony who had had the last laugh.

7: The Bailes 'Rumble'

Circuit of Britain, 1954
August 14th—23rd

Having lost the Brighton to Glasgow amateur event, the League were on the look out for another sponsor for an amateur event, and much to the disgust of the Union they had found one in the Southall company of Quaker Oats Ltd. The first Amateur Circuit of Britain struck an entirely new note for road-racing in this country. A stage race is not exactly a thing of joy to run and, before the advent of this event in 1954, there never had really seemed to be enough money.

For a stage race, other than the 'Tour of Britain', money just didn't grow on trees, and the stories of past events run with very, very little money, sheer showmanship and fantastic audacity, could very easily be the subject of another book.

Vic, the 'Humph', had learnt a lot from riding in League events and being Team Manager on the 'Peace Race', and we saw, sometimes for the first time, innovations in this race that had not been seen in this country before. Facilities such as advance baggage wagon; plastic bags for laundry; shoulder bags for personal clothing and, convoy control.

These innovations, and many others, went to make the race something worthwhile, not only from the riders' point of view, but from that of the officials as well. For them, there was the luxury of official cars that didn't look as though they were tied together with string. Hotels could be reached fairly easily and were comfortable – something which had not appeared in a race of this kind in Great Britain before.

The briefing for this first 'Humph' rough and tumble, for he was always a lad for going 'over the brown' on a map, took place in the hoko-poko land of Southall, close by the Quaker factory. It was in, to wit, Shackleton Road, and Victor, tubby lad that he is, let everyone, riders and officials alike, have it straight from the shoulder, and he certainly must have put it straight down the line, for there was no really serious infringement of the League and race regulations during the eight-day long race.

You could not wish for much more publicity than having the start of a stage race bang in the middle of a High Street on a Saturday morning, and Southall Park was jam-packed as the hour of eleven o'clock came round. There were no Indians to do a war-dance round the flag-pole, but T.V. personality, Sylvia Peters, without voice through laryngitis, was there to help the Mayor of Southall perform the rites of 'dropping the flag'.

Team Managers, bag carriers in those days, scurried around, trying to find out a bit more information than the next one. The Cyclo van was doing good business, albeit on the side, and without payment, while sundry junior tricyclists ran over everyone's tootsies and, to crown it all, after a really bad spell of weather, the sun was shining.

STAGE 1.   SOUTHALL TO NOTTINGHAM   137 MILES.
(AS THE CROW FLIES)

They were still sorting out the chaos left behind in the Uxbridge Road an hour after we had left, and to say that the traffic was closely packed would be to put it mildly. Through the Lady Margaret Road and out on to the Western Avenue we 'led out' and at Northolt Airport entrance we waved a yard or so of calico and they were away. Up Redhill in one big bunch they scurried and it's anchors away as they streaked down the hill, Amersham bound.

Through the leafy lanes of Buckinghamshire we ambled 25 m.p.h. being registered all the while, and Amersham was left behind and Wendover came and went, and a hard-working group of 17 crept off the front, and by Winslow, 40-odd miles they had a lead of 1 minute.

The undulating road took its toll, and group after group sort themselves out, found their place in life and settled down to make certain that they stayed there. In the meantime, up at the front, Bailes, Haskell, Carroll, Garvey, Kennedy, Armes, Evans and the other little nigger boys were blasting their way towards Nottingham and rest.

Through Wolston they flew and echeloned out round the sharp bends of Shilton, taking time out of the *peloton* all the while. Dicky Bowes of Yorkshire had bounced hard in the 'back-markers' and his 'Tour' was well and truly over. There were ten likely lads 'off the back' and with a bit of luck we would have been able to see them in Nottingham before lighting-up-time.

The leaders screamed down into Castle Donington and all arrived safely on the other side in one piece, but, on a fast stretch 2 miles further on, Lamb and Howarth played 'you touch me and I'll touch you' and slid a couple of hundred feet on their rumps, well and truly locked together.

This was the signal for an all-out sprint and the twelve who were left belted the daylights out of themselves, while Mick Howarth managed to grab Lamb's bike and give chase. There was a terrific 'bang' and Downham (Tame Valley) ate the dirt as his back tyre blew, and it was time for us to move up to the finish.

Such was the volume of traffic that we had to play 'dodgems' to get past, and just made the line before the leaders came into sight. It was Jock Kennedy (Scotland) who hit the corner first and, taking a long line from there, no-one got past and he became the first holder of the yellow jersey, from Frank Garvey (Manchester) and Alf Burford (Cambs. R.C.).

The rest scrambled in, in odd little bunches, but as late-duty timekeeper I had to wait for over an hour before the last man came in, and then found that there was no transport for me, and commenced a long walk into Nottingham. Luckily, the 'Jewel and Warris' outfit of Cyclo passed and so we lived for another day.

STAGE 2. NOTTINGHAM TO SCARBOROUGH 121 MILES.

There were 76 left in as they left the Pavilion in the Mansfield Road, knowing full well they would be in the thick of it within a very short while. As we climbed out of Nottingham, Tom Aldridge (Essex) was sick, and there was a gap of about 10 yards.

After Mansfield, anything went, and it was Brooke (Yorkshire) because his chain unshipped. A police car took up the race and four likely lads shed the rest and hared off up the road, with the police car playing 'Commissaire'. At Church Wallop they had a lead of 50 yards, and they were really cuckoo. When they got caught, they went to the back, and that was a fatal place to be in.

12 miles went and so had Armes, Mackin, Bailes, Downham and Ron Jowers, and the first 26 miles went by in 1 hour and 2 minutes. At Worksop they held a 50 second lead on Duffy, Hadlington and Greaves who had, in turn, 1 minute 50 seconds on the *peloton.*

They turned into a stiff wind, and Greaves punctured in both legs, while Duffy and Hadlington caught the five leaders after 14 hard miles of fierce struggle and graft. Through Doncaster they had a police escort and $4\frac{1}{2}$ miles the other side they had a lead of 2 minutes with Brian Haskell chasing like mad to make contact.

Jowers was ground into the dust and lost contact, while Haskell faltered and the bunch had him in its sights, and 3 peeled off and caught Brian just beyond Askern, but they were still $1\frac{1}{2}$ minutes behind the leaders. Coming up to the flats of Selby, Lee, Hetherington, Midgley, Burford and Brooke drew clear and inch by struggling inch they pulled back the leaders and before Selby was reached the leading group became nine, and they struggled on into the wind and the drizzling rain. Frank Garvey collected two kinds of 'parcels' and decided to send one home. Near Holme-upon-Spalding Moor, the leaders were $2\frac{1}{4}$ minutes up.

The leaders thrashed across the moors and began to break up. The wind strengthened and blew colder as they climbed the heights of Middleton-in-the-Wolds. As they pondered the heights to climb, up came Reg Browne, Frank Carroll, Frank Evans and Mick Howarth (Manchester), together with Tony Hewson, Geo. Downham, Eric Rowland and Arthur Hope.

The strain began to show and the *prime* just after Foxholes went to Tony Hewson (North Midlands), with Viv Bailes 2nd and Frank Evans, 3rd. It was a long, hard struggle to the top, then a hair-raising descent over the 'steppes' to Scarborough. It was one compact bunch that entered the town, seemingly hidden from the publicity that was rightfully theirs, and it was into a quiet back-water of the sea-side town that they turned.

Bailes was the first away and flew straight as a bird for the line. There was a bit of 'chopping' going on and the wheels 'pinged' as spokes were stretched taut. Elbows at the ready, they flashed towards the line and Duffy (Midlands) got the verdict from Reg Browne (Manchester) with Viv Bailes 3rd, but it was Bailes who now had possession of the race leader's banana-coloured jersey.

For the first time in this event a penalty was dished out and, Harry Bamforth (N.W. Region) copped 2 minutes for persistently riding on the wrong side of the road. Naughty Harry!

STAGE 3. SCARBOROUGH TO MORECAMBE 136 MILES.

The overnight head wind had changed and now hit the riders on their left shoulder. It was raining, and only five miles from Scarborough, Armes, Cubitt, Midgley, Jowers, Short and Hadlington had a short lead on the bunch, which at Pickering had become a minute.

Vic Stark went stark, staring mad and hurtled from the bunch and sped on his way to the leaders. As he reached them, Cubitt was dropped. They forced their way onwards at 28 m.p.h. and gradually increased their lead to 3½ minutes. The pace began to tell on one or two, and Midgley suddenly departed like a shot from a gun.

After the first foot-hills, they hammered down the notorious Sutton Bank, and in hair-raising fashion all managed to get down in one piece. Out on the Plain of York they stuffed food into pockets before getting down to climbing the real 'big stuff'.

At Thirsk, there were still only 3 in the lead, with the *peloton* at 4 minutes. At Pateley Bridge, thick mist made the going hectic, and Stark took the *prime* by 20 yards from Hadlington, with Short an also-ran. Milsom and Jowers were coming up behind. Down, down they screamed, reaching 50's in their anxiety to reach the bottom: a flock of sheep ambled out of the mist, Jowers hit one dead centre and luckily got off with just a broken arm.

Along the valley of Kilnsea they ambled losing Short and gaining Milsom, and it was 3 against a fast-moving bunch of 15, and it remained to be seen whether or not they could stay away to the finish. It is always a delight to see a mountain, to watch the sun chase the shadows across its face, but have you ever stopped to think how a racing cyclist views them? To him they mean a job of work, and he views them with a jaundiced eye. The agony is piled on as they reach the climb of Pen-y-Ghent, and their legs screamed for mercy as Stark again took the *prime*. A scuddering mist wafted across the grass-grown road down to Settle and Milsom sold out and went the way of all flesh, and the 2 who were left, Stark and Hadlington, being on their jack, made it easily to the bottom, while the bunch coming up behind chivvied about at sixes and sevens.

How they worked these 2! Bit and bit, bit and bit and, with 10 miles still to go the lead was now 1 minute 50 seconds. Right through Lancaster town they hurried, out on to the coast road and with only a few miles to go. Tension grew in the car for it had been an almighty duel covering over 100 miles. The run-in boards read it off for us; 4 to go; 3 to go; until we saw the ½ mile board.

Momentarily they sat up, shook hands, and the last round of this great struggle commences. They flew like homing pigeons along the sea-grit front and it was after the 200 yards flag that Vic Stark 'kicks'. Hadlington got out of his saddle, but had made the fatal mistake of being in too high a gear. Stark went and went and on the line he had it by two lengths. Suddenly a photographer kneeling in the middle of the wide road jumped to his feet and tried to jump back, but it was too late. He catches Vic's 'bars with his coat and swung him sideways and there, after the wonderful effort up hill and down dale, lay Stark, injured . . . and the rain poured down.

Just 2 minutes and 33 seconds later, sixteen more pound in, and it was over 1 hour and 40 minutes before Brian Hier tottered across the line. Twenty-one riders are packed into seventeen minutes so that it was still a very open race, and Viv Bailes still had the *maillot jaune*.

STAGE 4. MORECAMBE TO RHYL 118 MILES.

It was a blustery sort of day as the 70 left in line up, but there was a good crowd at the Pier Forebay to cheer them on their way. Vic Humphrey was charging around trying to find the character who had telephoned him at 2 a.m. as a practical joke, and luckily, he never did find him!

Out on the A.589 we let 'em go, and they raced through

Lancaster as though the Sheriff was after them. As they sped through Garstang, Gregg and Dunphy got tailed off, and Baker (Lincs) punctured. Two breaks had gone, 5 in the first and 3 in the second. Just outside Preston there was a strong cross-wind with stinging rain to boot, and the two breaks join and have a 30 second lead.

Coming up to Wigan Pier, Viv Bailes punctured, and the fireworks get going. Off set the bunch and by the time Newton-le-Willow was passed, Bailes was off the back to the tune of 1 minute 20 seconds, *and there was no-one around to help him!* Carroll, Evans, Baker and Haskell got with the leaders, while Bentley and Midgley got dropped.

At the feeding station at Hapsford, Clarke tried to get clear in the pouring rain, but nothing came of it, and it was Frank Carroll who took the Border *prime* from Haskell, with Bailes now well and truly in the mire to the tune of 4 minutes.

By Queensferry, the leaders were split into two groups and they looked a sorry sight in the torrential downpour, and Bailes had now dropped to 3rd on General Classification as he was over 6½ minutes down. Frank Garvey earned a name for himself by getting a 4 minute penalty for failing to stop at a Halt sign, and a Team Manager who asked a group of schoolkids on a corner, 'Anyone away?' got the reply, 'Sure mate, muvver's gone to Blackpool for the day.'

The Gwernmynydd *prime* ran water 2 to 3 inches deep as they splashed their way to the top. Carroll took it, sploshing his wheel just in front of Haskell's. The sudden drop down the other side sent them reaching for brakes, but luckily there was no hair-pin, and they all got down safely.

With 2 miles to go, Tony Hewson spread his wings and soon the leaders looked as though they are doing six solo runs-in, and it went on like this right to the line, with Hewson beating Mackin by 15 seconds, and he beat Evans by 2 seconds, while Lee crashed on the run-in.

The rest of the swimmers sloshed in with Bailes at 7 minutes 21 seconds, and he did not rate his chances much. One and a half hours later, Dunphy who 'blew' at Garstang rattled in, and that was the whole party of 68 complete for the day, with Frank Carroll (Manchester) now in the yellow jersey.

119

There were one or two minor misdemeanours and Brian Coombes copped two minutes, and Mackin and Carroll each got 30 seconds for throwing away a musette (in those days, valued beyond price!).

STAGE 5. RHYL TO ABERYSTWYTH   105 MILES.

No rain, but a sea-mist blowing in off the breakers as we started the 5th stage. After only 4 miles they began to drop off, and Brian Hier had the first 'drop', followed by Stonex (North London), then Hetherington and Bradshaw. The mist still hung like a giant clammy hand all around and it was difficult to see the riders.

At Llanwrst, the field began to spread out and suddenly, there was a gap, and everyone immediately began to look the worse for wear. On they go through the tranquil, most picturesque, wooded and hilly country to be found hereabouts, and so twisting were the lanes that it was difficult to tell where the leaders were and where the tail-end was.

There came a short preliminary hill, and the hill-climbers show their prowess . . . dancing out of the saddle like ballerinas stuck for an idea. It was not steep this hill, and they were moving fast. Down, down they swooped, like homing pigeons, through tree-girt lanes, twisting and turning like a snakes and ladders game gone mad.

Through a lop-sided gate we trundled at Penmachno and up a narrow sheep track that took us over a mountain with shouting streams on each side. Puncture follows puncture, and car after car boils over and gets left behind, and it's Haskell who led by 50 seconds at the *prime*, followed by Mackin and Lee.

The gritted, wind-swept road to Bala is not appreciated, even although the sun does break through in spasms; it is bitterly cold. So cold, in fact, that organiser Vic broke off at Bala and loaded up his car boot with bottles of rum 'for the lads at the finish' Haskell now led by 1½ minutes.

The field was split, and split again into small groups, chasing, chasing, chasing, and never very certain, because of the mist, what they were chasing. From Bala we passed 12 groups before catching up with Mackin, Waterfield, Bailes, Godbeer, Stark, Hewson, Keenahan, Woodhouse, Evans, Carroll and Lee at Dolgelley, and

THE CIRCUIT OF BRITAIN - 1954

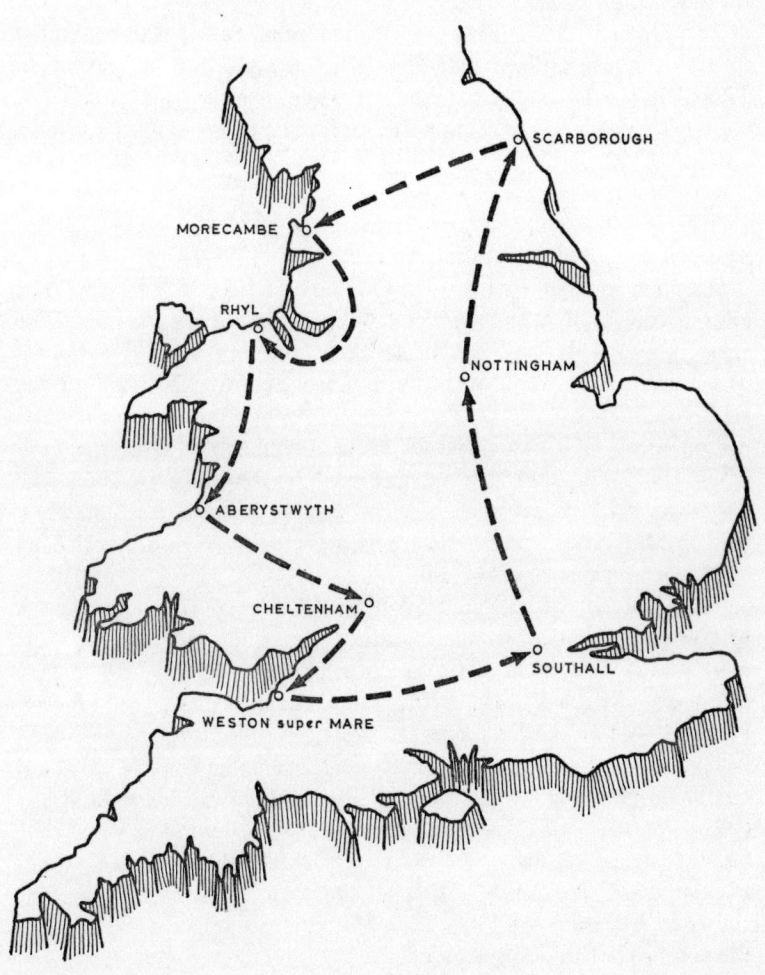

Haskell was finally caught, and Frank Carroll was able to breathe a sigh of relief.

Came the *prime* and it was Tony Hewson who 'took' Haskell on the line, only to be shot off on the run-in. Carroll, Stark and Mackin got involved in a crash that lost them valuable seconds as they negotiated the streets of Aberystwyth, and it was Frank Evans who came off best from Godbeer and Bailes. Brian Haskell got the yellow jersey by just a few seconds and no one was more surprised than Frank Carroll.

Everyone, of course, got their tot of rum, and it was beginning to get dark when Short and Hetherington ambled in to the finish. They'd had a stop at a cafe a little way out of town and had hot tea and cakes, before riding in to let us know that they were alright!

STAGE 6. ABERYSTWYTH TO CHELTENHAM 130 MILES.

Sunshine at last! A bit watery, but sunshine. Off we went, and after a couple of miles found we were all on the wrong road. The riders thoroughly enjoyed it as back through Aberystwyth we went, waving to the crowds once more, and we shot out on the right road.

The race got down to it in earnest when, just after the fork from Aber, the *prime* flag was espied. The Announcers' Car came up from behind and they told us that they were well on their way to Machynlleth and only realised that they were on the wrong road when no one caught them!

They played 'Music while you work' over the Tannoy, but it was not appreciated by the sweating, struggling riders, and Short and Stonex told them what to do with their wireless set as they came off the back. Again the rains came and all the officials hurriedly put on their duck feet.

The long-drawn-out-field showed as a long line of brilliant colour brightening a dull atmosphere, and it was Haskell of the yellow jumper who took the *prime* from Hewson. Down they hurtled over wooded hills with grey-faced sheep dotted about like so many mole-hills. Through the grey, stark valley out into the hills we went, and it's tiny Manns who broke away just as the sun broke through the clouds.

The Bailes 'Rumble'

After the hair-raising descent to Llanidloes, Manns is caught by Coombes and Lee and they led by a mere $\frac{1}{2}$ minute. They descended into the depths at Twylch and it was Lee who took the *prime* by 40 seconds from Manns and Coombes.

At Rhayader there was chaos when there was no marshal to point the way, and riders went both sides of the memorial but all came out safely on the other side. Came the climb of Radnor Forest and Lee was pulled back, and Mackin chopped down to take a crafty *prime* with Hodgson taking 2nd place. They had a 50 second lead, but another group could be seen coming up hotly.

Brian Haskell was somehow 2 minutes behind and by the time Hereford was reached it was 4 minutes, and the leading break consisted of Lee, who took the Border *prime*, Hewson, Hodgson, Harbottle, Mackin, Coombes, Bailes, Godbeer, Nowell and Turner. At the top of the hill outside Hereford, Manns, Armes and Garvey get up there and Bailes, now the leader, was up at the front of the bunch working like mad.

At Ross, with only a few 'pimples' to negotiate, Haskell was out the back to the tune of $4\frac{1}{2}$ minutes and Bailes could already feel that yellow jersey resting on his shoulders once again. It was here that the Cyclo van, following the leaders a bit too closely, took a sharp-left-hander and found itself suddenly in the middle of a churchyard.

The run-in was not of the best and a group of 16 could take up a lot of road. Apart from one or two people having the scare of their lives, and the odd car or so pulling up a bit smartish, nothing much happened, and the whole bunch turned into Lansdown Road for the gallop.

Brian Coombes had bigger elbows than the rest and got the verdict, but Tony Hewson was able to chop down hard and so get 2nd place from Godbeer, with all the other jolly little sailor-boys at the proverbial fag-paper. Garvey again ran foul of official-dom and another minute went on his time for throwing away his musette, while Stratford got 2 minutes for letting his musette obscure his number.

Viv Bailes had the *maillot jaune* back as Haskell came in nearly $8\frac{1}{2}$ minutes down. The late duty timekeeper and judge had another long wait of over an hour for Rudd, Stonex, Endruweit and

123

Hadlington, but at least they had the decency to let us know that they had finished.

STAGE 7. CHELTENHAM TO WESTON SUPER MARE   101 MILES.

We started the stage with the climb of Birdlip, and none of the riders gave any 'lip' to any 'bird', 'cos they were all working too hard! It was a long, stiff pull up and, as they left the *prime* point, taken by Mackin, they stretched and stretched and stretched out in a long colourful line, dominated by the figure of Bailes, with his bright yellow jersey in the lead.

Coombes obviously liked to be on his own, so scurried off down the road and at Tetbury led by 40 seconds, with Bailes doing all the work at the front of the bunch. Without much effort they pulled Brian back just as they entered Malmesbury, and the whole field went off course (twice round the market square) by kind (!) permission of a policeman!

Rain was falling heavily as at Melksham, Harbottle, Coombes and Keenahan took the lead-pole and the Farleigh *prime* goes to Harbottle. Along the narrow, mud-strewn lanes they hurtle and Keenahan punctured and then had gear and brake trouble. It was only the watchfulness of the G.B. Service car that got him going again.

On the last *prime* at Bleadon, Harbottle took the lead as Coombes fumbled his gear change and, when they hurtled down the other side, Coombes hurtled through a farmhouse door, when his over-zealousness made him brake suddenly, and he slipped on some cows' 'whatsit' on the hair-pin bend. They pulled him out, chucked a bucket of water over him, and pushed him off at the end of a long pole!

It is Harbottle who went on to win the stage, never having won a race before in his life! The leaders came in, not too far down, and the also-rans were still running an hour after Harbottle had been in.

The only good thing about the day was that Coombes got a 30 second bonus, which is the time he was in advance when the bunch was directed off course. Even good came out of it sometimes!

124

STAGE 8. WESTON SUPER MARE TO LONDON (SOUTHALL) 149 MILES.
'Waste of time,' someone in the crowd said, 'Bailes can't possibly
lose with 4 minutes in hand.' That was the comment of most, and
the start was preceded by all the foolishness that typifies the
start of the last day of a great stage race. Comic hats were seen
around; pictures taken from the most improbable places; even Vic
had a smile on his face, and everyone was of the opinion that it
was all over bar the shouting.

Of course, the race had had its humorous moments – what stage
race hasn't? At Rhyl, Vic and I had a rare old time at 2 o'clock
in the morning, going in and out of various bedrooms, in search
of feeding bottles and musettes, and finding out they weren't all
riders' rooms either! Then there was Des Robinson and his
whistle. He used it to scare sheep on the mountain stages, and
believe it or not, he was nearly 'rammed' once or twice.

Well, there we were, on the sea-front at Weston, the mountains
and the so-called tough stages behind us, and all set for a joyous
run home. The sun shone, the crowds appeared in their thousands,
and there were still 53 riders left to contest the last stage.

Down went the flag and away they went. We hopped in the car,
hopped out again, got the keys out of the boot lock, and then could
not get away for the traffic. We got stopped at traffic lights, held
up at cross-roads by a copper, and finally made to the front of
the field at Locking.

As we scrambled over the bridge a figure crept away from the
bunch and we're at it again. Another jumped the gun and the 2
got together and disappeared into the distance. Dave Lee and
Derek Worsley had taken their departure.

Vic made his decision and we stayed with the bunch. At
Churchill cross-roads we had fun, for three mobile marshals went
towards Bristol, while the rest of us turned right towards Cheddar.
The field went so slow that 6 got tangled up going up a slight
rise. No one was hurt, except pride.

They all made the Gorge safely and commenced the climb. A
geezer in a Standard 10 thought it was a great game and held the
field up while he played 'peek-a-boo'. We get past him firmly and
not very politely, and left the riders behind. We catch Lee and
Worsley, sucking oranges happily. They now have a $6\frac{1}{2}$ minute
lead.

We got out to admire the scenery at Chelwood and as the 2 fugitives went by I give them the high sign that they have nearly 10 minutes' lead. Dave scratched what he called a head and they got down to it. The field came by at last and Vic told them in no uncertain terms that he'd stop their tea-money if they didn't get cracking, and they cheerfully gave him the razz.

Soon after Marksbury, Ted Lees, the official photographer, had an argument with a big, black bull, and it took the efforts of half-a-dozen officials to get him off. Then Humphrey tried his hand at an aria from Carmen, and the merry bunch 'took the mickey'. We caught the flying pair on the outskirts of Bath and both still looked very cheerful.

We waited in a lay-by and it was 12 mintues before the *peloton* came by, and Mike Matthews was on the tail, making signs that his freewheel was beginning to freewheel both ways, and that he was going ahead to get it changed. The Cyclo van screamed past the bunch and the wheel was changed in double quick time, but Mike was now some 15 seconds down. We ambled through Bath, giving the locals the griff on the Tannoy of what it was all about.

On the corner of the A.4 we espied a yellow-jerseyed, imploring, gesticulating figure, *a la Bartali*. 'Please, please give me a wheel,' came the cry, and Viv Bailes' hands plead in supplication as our car slowly passed him.

The Gnutti van crash-stopped half on and half off the pavement, and half-a-dozen willing hands reached out to help. We cleared a way through the mass of cars and 5, 10, 15, 25 seconds went by before Bailes appears. The field were still in sight, but were beginning to move fast as they realised that Bailes was no longer with them.

Mike Matthews reached us first and Vic told him the situation. He sat up, looked round, and waited. Bailes steamed up, sweat already bursting in great bubbles from his forehead. A rider detached himself from the *peloton* ahead, turned round and came back. It was Bennett, a team-mate of Bailes. By the time we reached Batheaston the 3 were moving well together, but the main bunch were moving even faster.

We wished Bailes luck and moved on to the bunch. At Box we learnt that Lee had taken the *prime* and he now led on the 'King of the Mountains' section. We waited and checked. Haskell was

first up, followed by Godbeer, Hewson and Mackin. They re-
grouped and away they went. Bailes broke the top first, but it was
$1\frac{1}{2}$ minutes since the bunch had gone. We fell in behind and
instructed them to change at every 100 yards. They did, but the
pace began to tell and soon Bennett 'blew' completely and though
he fought hard he never made it back.

The field by this time was really steaming, and they dropped
into Chippenham like so many stones. They threaded their way
through the mid-day traffic and, regrouping, proceeded to eat road.
We checked again on the outskirts and Matthews and Bailes came
through $2\frac{1}{2}$ minutes down.

It was now serious and we by-passed the riders to drown our
sorrows on the downfall of a great rider at a pub at Beckhampton.
The bunch drifted past and we raised our glasses in salute. A wait
of $3\frac{1}{4}$ minutes and along came the tandem. We lowered our glasses
and commiserated that it was virtually all over.

At the top of Marlborough Hill we made another check and
the time stood at 3 minutes 50 seconds, and Bailes had lost his
lead to Derek Evans by 10 seconds. The streaky, white salt marks
stood out grimly on Bailes' face and there was a steady trickle of
sweat from his chin. Lanky Mike Matthews looked all-in, grey-
faced but still moving. They paired up again, like the parts of a
machine coming together, and changed every 100 yards or so. It
was nearly all downhill to Froxfield and their whirling pedals took
them through the 30's into the 40's and 50's as they skimmed over
the ground.

As they hurtled round the right-hander at Froxfield at amazing
speed the tail-end of the *peloton* was seen breasting the hill. There
was the 'Three Sisters' between Froxfield and Hungerford and, as
Bailes and Matthews switchbacked up and down, each rise saw
the field getting nearer and nearer. Bailes now had the bit between
his teeth, and those legs that had carried him round for eight days
on this Circuit of Britain now began to pump up and down like
pistons.

We reached the outskirts of Hungerford to the cheers of all the
officials in the following cars. Viv and Mike scented their prey
and, on a long, long swoop down, made contact. Matthews thankfully sat in on the back of the bunch while Viv Bailes went to
the front, his yellow jersey awash with perspiration.

127

This was what stage racing was all about. Here we had a long hard chase of 45 sun-blessed, undulating, soul-searching miles, but grit, guts, determination, plus the help of a lad, Mike Matthews, who had, in his own words, 'Been about to pack', had got Bailes back to the bunch.

Lee and Worsley were back in the bunch and, over at Stokenchurch the *prime* was battled out by Hewson and Hodgson with the 'bite' going to Hodgson. In High Wycombe came chaos with traffic and lights and eight 'made a date' with the finish at Southall. Dark-skinned little Laurie Manns is at the front, taking flyers off of all and sundry, and Beaconsfield came and went before the last stretch down the Western Avenue and home.

Five, in Manns, Hewson, Routledge, Coombes and Nowell battled it out for the honour of winning the last stage and it was Coombes that got pipped on the line by tiny Manns who thrusted himself forward with his last ounce of strength.

It was all over, with Viv Bailes winning by 3 minutes and 48 seconds from Evans, with Haskell a mere 42 seconds away in 3rd place. The team race was won by Lakeland, from Tees-side and the Midlands, while Dave Lee was 'King of the Conks' from Tony Hewson and Haskell. Altogether 52 finished.

But although it had been a wonderful week, I still think of the great but unfortunate riders who fell by the wayside, some of them literally. Of them all, I shall remember most of all Geof Downham, blood streaming from shoulder to fingertips, getting back on his bike and riding on, and on, and on, until stopped by Vic Humphrey, and being virtually carried to the ambulance.

This was surely a tribute to a great race.

Desmond Robinson beating Alan Jackson by 'a lick of paint' into
Glasgow on Stage 4, Circuit of Britain 1955

Brian Haskell, reduced to walking for
the first time in his cycling career in
Stage 6, Circuit of Britain, 1955

Gil Taylor leads Bill Bradley over the Butterbubs on Stage 2 of the 1956 Circuit of Britain

Timekeepers and judges view the scene as Doug. Collins (Army) takes the last stage at Worthing on the 1956 Circuit of Britain

8: Pure 'Circus'

Circuit of Britain, 1955
July 15th—23rd

There were no bands playing, or flags flying in Manchester on Thursday, 14th July, 1955, yet at Chorlton Town Hall there was a gathering of over 300 people. Coming from all walks of life, colourful in themselves, yet with a tension about them that spoke of things yet to come. There was a sprinkling of newspaper men but very few of the general public present.

8 days before, in Paris, the 'controle' had been crowded with thousands of people, just waiting to catch a glimpse of the famous riders signing in for the world-famed, professional, 'Tour de France'.

Here in England, in Manchester, there was a gathering of amateur riders. The finest and best amateur riders in the country, quietly signing in and collecting their numbers, their laundry bags and the sundry items that went to make up the day to day kit of the 'Tour' man. To watch them gave one a quiet pride in the fact that there was no rowdiness, just a fellow feeling of comradeship and goodwill.

They were there to contest the second Amateur Circuit of Britain – 'The Oats' to you, and run under the regulations of the British League of Racing Cyclists. Victor George Humphrey, the organiser, had planned a route that put all others to shame. Moorland and mountains, hills and dales, scenery good enough to bless the eyes of all who see it – but not many of these riders would see any of it during the next nine days. They would be too busy watching the coloured jerseys of the riders in front, or trying to calculate in their minds how far the *peloton* is behind.

E   129

'You have 1,066 miles in front of you – tough ones,' they were told by Vic, before they went off to their hotels to spend a restless night dreaming of the morrow.

At the crack of dawn off went the pathfinder team to put up the arrows marking the route, and slowly things began to stir. Officials and riders began to assemble at Whitworth Park; mechanics tinkered with machines; managers rubbed legs; panic abounds as someone found they had left something behind at the hotel. Everything gradually came into perspective and riders lined up ready for the Lord Mayor of Manchester to drop the starting flag.

STAGE 1. MANCHESTER TO SCARBOROUGH 147 MILES.

Writing the story of the first stage of the 1955 'Oats' is to write an epic! Here was the 'Tour de France' come to life in England, and with typical 'Tour' scenery. The sun was already hot, and listless clouds of grimy smoke hung heavily in the air as the riders were given the '5, 4, 3, 2, 1, GO' at 10.45 a.m.

From Whitworth Park they wended their way through the teeming 'Saturday morning' Manchester City traffic and out, after devious backstreets, on to the Oldham Road. The neutralising flag hung starkly red and white in the shimmering heat haze, and the inside of our car was already like a furnace. They ambled along, waving to the thousands that lined the sidewalks. Up to the fork in the Oldham Road trundled the gaily coloured spectacle; toestraps were tightened; jerseys made comfortable; many started jockeying for position; the red and white flag was hauled in and replaced by one with a black border . . . the race was on!

In a sense, this was a lesson from which we all learned something, for the lads took it easy, sensing that to show their loyalty to the League, the Rules of the road must be obeyed, and although the pace got steadily faster, it was done without undue hurry. At Rochdale, Paddy Boyd (Army C.U.) had a spot of gear trouble and the Cyclo van whipped up smartly and its crew soon had him on his way back to the bunch.

At Bacup, the pace was beginning to tell and the field was stretched way out. Nearing the hill-top we found that Taylor and Gregory (Wales) had been 'tailed-off' and we P.A. them, trying to get them back to the bunch. The run down was terrific and Gregory took the second corner much too fast, and then . . . over a 3 ft wall he went, then over the top of a 12 ft mound, turning slowly over and over in the air. We crash-stopped and raced towards him even before he touched down. As we reached him he was rising to his knees. He shook his head mightily, sighed, and said 'Crikey, I never made that one.'

Cyclo got him on his way and by fast motoring we caught the field at Hebden. Just out of the town came the first *prime* of the Circuit, the heart-rending, soul-searing climb of Pecket Well. 7 miles in length, the first ¾-mile was cobble-covered with an average gradient over the whole length of 1 in 7.

As they rounded the first corner there was a pile-up and Viv. Bailes, the 1954 Winner came off, and stood there helplessly waiting for another wheel. Only with skilful driving did we get past and just reached the *prime* point in time to see Carroll (Manchester) take it from Browne and Haskell. By now, the remainder of the riders were just so many coloured dots bobbing up and down on the hill. A re-grouping went on on the descent, while we held up the convoy so that all should have a safe passage down.

Through Shipley and Otley they hammered, and the field was constantly being split up. Viv Bailes had got back somehow, but punctured, got back on, punctured again, and was destined to spend much of the rest of the day alone.

The groups were moving fast as they approached Blubberhouses – delightful to tourists – and many riders formed up to make sizeable bunches. There were miniature hair-pins; descents; climbs and bends; the descents were awe-inspiring and the tiny fragments of colour dropped down to be lost in the whole colourful mass of the scenery like little tiny coloured beetles trying to crawl up the face of a wall. The sun blazed down, and climb, descent, and the hot sun, began to take their toll.

Up at Pateley Bridge the leading bunch included Jock Kennedy, Des Robinson, Derek Evans, Dick Bartrop, Ed Penvose and Swinney. The well-spread-out feeding station came as a welcome relief and here we learnt that Bailes was way down to the tune of *45 minutes.*

As they sped through the market place of Ripon they were

131

beginning to look the worse for wear, and Thirsk really made 'em 'thirsky' and a number of riders poured whole bottles of water over their heads. Clubfolk were out in their hundreds and sponges and bottles were bandied about, left, right and centre.

The 6-man break began to break and then came Sutton Bank, that 1 in 4 son of Yorkshire, that set Jock Kennedy 'dancing a reel' that the others with him could not match. He jerked at the pedals, he swayed hither and yon, he stamped and sweated, but he was relentless, and at the top he had a lead of 50 seconds over young Swinney of Exeter, who was followed up by Penvose. Bartrop managed to get back with the leaders again, having broken his rear spindle and changed his bike at the bottom of the hill.

The rest of the field were spread-eagled from here back to Ripon, and while they trundled towards the 'Bank', Jock Kennedy took flight and hammered at a 39 mile time-trial towards the finish at Scarborough. Between him and a chasing group of four was Swinney, still turning 'em round with the best, but Jock was moving even faster, for he dropped down through Helmsley and Pickering gaining seconds on everyone with every mile.

Crowds lined the route on the run-in to Scarborough and round the wide sweep of the North Bay he travelled, getting a tremendous reception all the way. Nearly $5\frac{1}{2}$ minutes after he crossed the line, 4 more pounded across with Des Robinson getting 2nd place from Bartrop, Evans and Penvose, while young Swinney crawled in a further $1\frac{1}{2}$ minutes down.

It had been a tough day's racing, and 71 did well to finish, only Park (R.A.F.) coming out with a strained thigh muscle.

STAGE 2. SCARBOROUGH TO WHITLEY BAY 112 MILES.

The Mayor of Scarborough performed the honours on the Marine Parade, and Jock Kennedy en-robed in the first *maillot jaune* of the race leader. The heat was terrific as we left Scarborough's Bay behind, but as soon as the flag went down a fast moving group departed helter-skelter from the bunch.

An undulating road took us through Whitby and after 9 miles there was a definite break: Jock Kennedy, not being with it, began to look a mite worried. He had reason to be, for he wasn't to see them again until after the finish at Whitley Bay!

Water buckets and sponges were much in evidence, while a couple of team cars joined in and began to boil a bit in the blazing heat. Anything went for a team car, and a real right lot of 'old bangers' some of them were.

The pace went on relentlessly, a neat average of between 22 and 23 m.p.h. showing on our speedo all the while. Tony White (London) had knee trouble and although he struggled gamely on, he had to give up in the end and climb into the back of the large white, cool, Aspro ambulance.

After 41 miles, at Guisborough, the leading group numbered 15, and no more riders were ever to make it to the break. Tweddell (Army C.U.) tries, and did a lone 50 miles out and out effort, which cost him stacks of energy and got him exactly nowhere.

The people of Middlesbrough were out in their hundreds and Bailes, with the lead group was cheered again and again. Through Stockton, Sedgfield, Coxhoe and Durham they sped, and the story remained the same. A 'flat-out' 100 yards at the front and then back at the rear. It was monotonous, regular as clockwork, but paying huge dividends.

Behind them the field was splitting up gradually due to the fast pace, the heat, and the fact that, try as they might, they were making no impression whatsoever on the leaders. A little light relief came at Witton Gilbert, where we had the feeding station, when Wren (North Central) was spied sitting on the top of a horse-trough with his feet in the water, and declaring to all and sundry that he was not going to move another inch until his 'plates of meat' had cooled off!

Across the Anfield Plain, the heat rises in haze from the road, and the leaders, now down to ten sweating racing boys, consists of clown Baty, Hewson, Stratford, Penvose, Ward, Taylor, Robinson, Holliday, Bailes and Browne. They pounded the living daylights out of themselves and, nearing his home town, Bill Baty slipped the leash, took a flyer and lengthened the gap with each thrust of his legs. With 105 miles covered, he screamed through Two Ball Lonnen with a lead of $1\frac{1}{2}$ minutes and looked like staying out there until the finish.

The mileages seemed to have been calculated 'as the crow flies' and none of these lads bore any resemblance to crows. 9 chased one and cramp played its part and Bill got pulled back at Earsdon, with only 8 miles to go. At Front Street we got a shock when we found that the routeing van had failed to take a bend and was having a 'rest' on its side, but sharp manipulation by all concerned made certain that the arrows were out on the final 5 mile run-in.

We entered Whitley Bay on 'Carnival Day' to the thunderous cheers of 100,000 people and to parades, banners and waving flags. There were minutes of tension as the way was cleared and the yellow flag was raised giving the signal that the riders were coming.

10 sweating, pounding couriers heaved their way towards the line. Ken Stratford (North West) got out in front, hotly pursued to the line by the other nine. The crowds loved it, and shouted themselves hoarse, and it was Stratford who got the verdict from Dick Bartrop and Ray Holliday. Kennedy came in 11 minutes and 32 seconds down, and it was Dick Bartrop who now had the race leadership, and 3 more went on the 'retired' list.

STAGE 3.   WHITLEY BAY TO MUSSELBURGH   133 MILES.

Outside the Rex Hotel, the Cyclo men were sweating it out just before the start of this stage, for today the race went over the Cheviot and Moorfoot Hills. A lot of care and attention was given to gears for the team-cars had to hot-foot it, before the start, to a point 30 miles out, for a supplementary feed, due to the heat.

At the flag they were at it again, just as though the finish were just around the corner and not, in fact, 130 rugged miles away. It was slightly cooler, but the lads sensed speed and all breaks were pulled back. It must have been heartbreaking at the front for our speedo showed a regular 28 m.p.h. The road swung and with hardly a flat mile the riders got buffeted by an unhelpful wind across the moorlands, and the tail-end began to wag. Through Moorpeth to Hartburn – and many were the hearts that were burning on this day. Each town, each village, had its quota of people out and even whole schools were out with teachers leading the cheering.

After 30, thirsty, dusty miles, the break came. 8 sweat-streaked souls crept away from the bunch, a corner hid them, and they were gone. We went on light-heartedly to discover Jimmy Saville singing to some cows in a field, and we heard later that 1 had died of shock!

Up Carter Bar we cruised and the 6 had a 1 minute 20 second lead. Kennedy sought some light relief and left the second group to pound itself into the dust and departed, together with wheel-sucking Paddy Boyd, and rangy Gil Taylor. So fast did they travel that the 6 leaders were passed and it was Kennedy who whipped the Carter Bar *prime* from under Paddy Boyd's nose.

Down to Hawick we motored fast but we never saw the leaders. The sun chased shadows across the foothills of Scotland and many a tired rider turned a bleary eye on the gorgeous scenery. At the Robertson feeding station, the cry was 'water' – water in sponges, bottles and even buckets!

Ray Holliday, on holiday from the R.A.F., came through in company with Robinson and Penvose, 2 clear minutes in front of a lively group of seven. At a further ½ minute there was a group of 13 and the main *peloton* is a bedraggled 8 minutes away. But the way was still hard and weary. We swept down to Tushielaw, and we crept up and slithered down to Traquair. The leading group had become 10 at Innerleithen.

Came the last climb over Whitehope Law and Ladyside Height, and Bristow took his departure from the back. Gil Taylor walloped a large stone a terrific bang and damaged both wheels. At the top, Penvose let a gap appear – and then there were 7. Still they pounded on, with Penvose grinding his teeth and working himself to a standstill, but he just could not get back on.

They scurried through Dalkeith and into Musselburgh, and there was no let-up even to the line. The tremendous effort showed in faces, bodies, taut-muscles and legs begrimed in sweat and dirt. It was Holliday who streaked through to take the stage by a length from Paddy Boyd (Army C.U.) with Des Robinson, half a length away, third, but he now had the yellow jersey.

STAGE 4. EDINBURGH TO GLASGOW   57 MILES.

It was cold, damp and miserable for the start of this so-called 'rest' day. Add to this the fact that a number of riders and officials couldn't find the start, and it seemed that we are all set for a real right time.

Through central Edinburgh we trundled and at Sighthill, 4 miles out, we let them go, and immediately Jackson, Shepherd, Bailes,

Holliday, Ross, Robinson, Boyd, Tweddell and Goddard got away. Only a mere gap at first, but it widened as backs were bent in endeavour and pedals thrust down. Through West Calder they galloped, tyres humming a song of triumph. Boyd was shed as he punctured in both lungs. Goddard had death in his legs and came off soon after, grey-faced and haggard. At 20 soul-searing miles, the lead was a minute and had been well earned.

Evans (Wolverhampton) sensed danger and screamed off the bunch with Kennedy, Brackstone (London) and Browne (Manchester) and 5 others hot-footing up to the leaders, but the chase was to last until the finish.

At Cleghorn Station, the level-crossing gates closed *behind* the leaders, and for the chasers the halt was but a moment as the friendly 'keeper' opened the side gates and let them through. The advantage was slight – about 5 seconds. At Lanark came a HALT sign and everyone touched down nicely – thank you very much. Brackstone is doing his nut, together with Kennedy, Browne and Evans, but they are banging their heads against a brick wall.

Tweddell came off the back as though pushed with a giant hand and, as we approached the finish, the sky was grey, overcast and foreboding. They bounced across a cobbled stretch and it looked as though a slow-moving car might baulk them, but it was moved on by the police just in time and, at the line, it was Des Robinson by a lick of paint from Jackson (Army C.U.) with Ray Holliday, a fag-paper away, 3rd.

So jubilant was Des that, what with pressmen and photographers he forgot to hand in his neck tally and was penalised a minute, but still remained race leader.

STAGE 5.   GLASGOW TO CARLISLE   120 MILES.

64 riders started in brilliant sunshine from Glasgow Green and, from their pace one would think they were but having a spin round the houses and even before 5 miles have gone, Summers (B.U.C.U.) found the pace too hot and left the field for the comforts of the 'meat wagon'. Bill Baty, the grave-digging clown, punctured in both legs, with only 8 miles covered.

The work of the Yorkshiremen was really impressive for every break, or vestige of a break was covered. Gino Goddard (London)

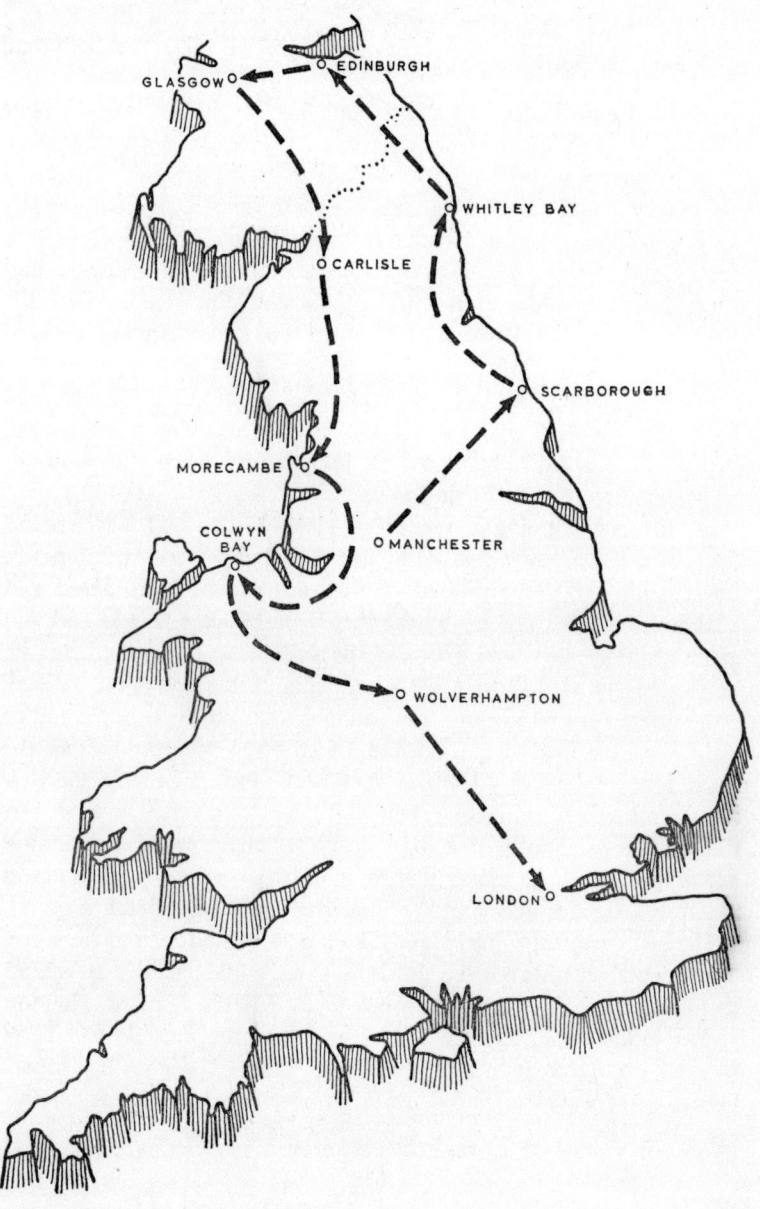

THE CIRCUIT OF BRITAIN - 1955

GLASGOW

EDINBURGH

WHITLEY BAY

CARLISLE

SCARBOROUGH

MORECAMBE

COLWYN
BAY

MANCHESTER

WOLVERHAMPTON

LONDON

brought fame upon his head when he belted across a HALT sign at Rosebank and earned himself a 5 minute penalty. At Kirkfieldbank came a short, stubborn and twisting climb and they let off steam and tiny drops of colour left the bunch and became distinguishable as reds, and blues, and greens – and the field had been split.

'Jock' Kennedy led the attack, followed by Carroll and Browne (Manchester). They regrouped at the top and sped on their way. The pattern was forming. At Abington, Brian Haskell was away on his own and he climbed the Menock Pass easily and steadily with a group, including Kennedy, Robinson and Evans, never very far behind. It was hot, it was tough, completely unsheltered, and there was 1,500 feet of it, right up to Wanlock Head, where the highest houses in Britain look down on the menacing face of Menock.

Coming along behind, Bristow and Neal (South-East) and Collinson (South-West) missed the arrows and the marshal and, instead of bearing right, hared off into the unknown and were not to be seen again until the finish.

At the *prime* point it was Brian Haskell who had a 50 second lead, and it was near this point that Viv Bailes ran 'out of road', hit a bank and somersaulted 20 foot down a ravine! Dazed and shaken he was picked up by the Aspro ambulance people and was given medical attention. His was the spirit that never died, for he recovered sufficiently to insist on finishing the stage. Viva Bailes!

14 riders formed up into the leading group on the descent and at the Closeburn feeding station had a lead of $3\frac{1}{2}$ minutes with all the main race leaders way back at 7 minutes. Jock Kennedy, the first into Scotland, must have taken a dislike to his native land for, despite the attentions of a giant lorry which impeded the leading group for miles, he cleverly won the border *prime* from Jackson at Gretna Green, and was the first man *out* of Scotland.

Haskell, Kennedy, Perks and Sanderson turned on the pressure. They raced on towards the finish as though 'old Nick' was behind them and daylight showed between them. Morris, Browne, Hewson and Tweddell took up the chase and the gap was closed. They weaved and changed, and there was more daylight. By superhuman efforts it was closed again and again. Haskell was bleary-eyed but still ready to have a go. Dowling looked all in and hung on the back like grim death. It was a do or die effort and the strain was terrific. 7 long and lonely minutes behind there was an 'express train' with Goddard, Brackstone, Boyd and Armitage thrashing themselves silly to catch the leaders.

The excitement of the chase mounted with each passing second. The wheels sung as they raced down the hill towards the old world town of Carlisle. In line abreast they screamed towards the finishing line. It was Perks, it was Kennedy, it was Sanderson. Each and every one threw his bike in a frenzy of movement towards that tantalising line. It was the Judges job to sort them out, and the verdict went to Perks by a tyre from Sanderson, with Jock Kennedy rubbing noses with the two of them!

It was a further 6 minutes before the 'express' rolled in, and nearly 10 minutes went by before the *peloton* swept across the line, with Robinson still the race leader. The 3 'off-course' riders were given a 'token' time and so salved everyone's conscience.

STAGE 6.   CARLISLE TO MORECAMBE   118 MILES.

It was a two-part stage for the sixth day, and the first part was mainly an uphill time-trial to Lakelands tourist centre, Keswick and at 9.31 a.m. the first rider departed on his lone journey.

The course was only 36 miles in length, the first 19 being of billiard table smoothness, while the remaining 17 were a nightmare for the unwary. Jackson did the 'ride of his life' and clocked 1.33.07, while Haskell ploughed through Goddard, Richardson and Turner to take 2nd place with 1.34.29, with Ray Holliday, 3rd, only 10 seconds away.

A hasty, tasty meal was eaten before the Keswick Council Chairman sent them on their way for the second half of the nightmare and there was an *unexpected prime point* 3½ miles from the start in Keswick's market place when the Prime Judge's car broke down and somehow 'Fangio' Humphrey managed to get past the cursing riders, and the Newlands *prime* had still to be contested, and the riders got two *primes* for the price of one!

A silence hung heavily over the mountainside as rider after rider strained at the pedals, was baulked by the slow moving train in front, and eventually, fell in a slow moving curve to the ground. Ken Stratford broke a pedal. Don Blissett (London) hit a sheep dead-centre, and retired. Those in front had better fortune for they handled their machine with confidence and again it was Haskell, bidding for the 'King of the Mountains', who breasted the top first.

The blue jersey of Yorkshire swooped down from the mountains, skimmed the hair-pin corner at Buttermere and was gone. Seconds later, a white-jerseyed figure came hurtling down, followed by the blood-red of the King of the Mountains, braking and fighting a slipping, slithering, bucking broncho machine on the murderous corners. Another blue jersey rattled by – it was Penvose, doing his nut to catch the leaders. A few seconds more and the Yellow Jersey appeared, glasses glinting in the strong sunlight, face lined and dusty from the swirling clouds of dust sweeping up from the road. They rode with superb courage these amateurs, but courage was not enough, for there was always someone there to put the screws on.

Haskell hurried along narrow, grit-topped roads with severe bends and high stone walls with overhanging trees for company. In a few short miles came the back-breaking lung-torturing, soul-destroying, leg-wearying toil over the Honister Pass. It was bitterly cold on the mountain top, yet hot enough for a bikini in the valleys.

Brian climbed steadily and well, still clear of Kennedy and Evans, while Des Robinson showed signs of 'wear and tear' and, for the first time in 8 years of racing, *got off his bike and walked*. About ¼ mile from the summit, Haskell licked his lips, gave a twisted grin and left Evans and Kennedy looking as though they'd stopped. At the top he had a precious 45 seconds and Vic, ever partisan, told him to 'go, go, GO'. The descent spelt tragedy for him for he missed a bend and cooling river waters closed over him. He was just about to get out when Johnny Morris (Army C.U.) joined him. By the time they had found John's glasses in the water, they were 6 minutes down on the leaders.

Right along the lake of Derwentwater the field was spread out. Sanderson was in a group with Haskell; Carroll was in a group with Perks and Armitage, while Bailes, Kennedy, Boyd, Evans and Robinson had the leading group in their grip and dictated the policy.

At Ullswater, thousands were out to see the Campbell test for the water speed record. Our passing brings light to a dark day for them, for the lowering clouds make sombre patterns on the water. Kirkstone Pass was car-infested, from the humble 'baby' Austin to the huge Humber 'Snipe'. A car stalled and all hell was let loose as it began to run back, and riders gambled on getting through a gap 18″ wide and to safety on the other side. It was Short (North Central) who took the *prime* by 1¼ minutes from Boyd and Bailes.

We left Bailes far behind and coasted down this awe-inspiring drop at sixty-fives. Vivian was not to be outdone however for, as we approached the 'Mortal Man' Inn he left us behind as though we were standing still. Short was still away and moving nicely and he gained a slight advantage at Staveley when the level-crossing gates close behind him, but this was whittled away when at Kendal he got stopped at the traffic lights, and this evened things up a bit. It was at Carnforth that they finally caught him, and it was all over bar the shouting. Yorkshire were laughing their heads off for they had 3 men in the break. They sat, they watched, and the miles passed steadily.

And then, in a moment of passing time, the sea appeared and they were off their saddles and streaking for the line like so many coloured 'Sugar Puffs'. A heaving, struggling, colourful mass that broke up as it reached the finishing line and became placed as Des Robinson first, Neal (South-East) second, and Paddy Boyd, third, and Des was still the race leader.

STAGE 7.   MORECAMBE TO COLWYN BAY   117 MILES.

This stage provided the welcome and easy 'flat' route into Wales. It was hot and sticky, and petrol fumes made a blue haze on the A.6 as the riders sped along. It was flat and uninteresting, and yet it had its revelations.

For instance, in the Army team, Tweddell had trouble with his freewheel. The centre cog stripped – Cyclo's van was called and Bladon, Tweddell and the van all crash-stopped together. Bladon left his bike for Tweddell, who pounded away and got back to the bunch. Cyclo whipped a machine from the van and away went Bladon. He did his nut and made contact with the bunch. Cyclo fixed the freewheel, got ahead and pulled into a lay-by. Tweddell and Bladon jumped off their machines at the same time. Tweddell grabbed his and let Bladon's go. Bladon grabbed his and let Cyclo's machine go. In 2 seconds they were away and only 30 yards separated them from the bunch. Nice work, Army!

It was a 9 day wonder how some of these lads kept going! Taylor and Wilkinson of Wales for instance, must have ridden hundreds of miles on their own, yet we timekeepers knew that, no matter how late it was, they would come rolling in, and Taylor would have a grin as huge as any Cheshire cat.

Just before Wigan they began to get cracking, and a useful gap was opened up by Dowling, Short, Boyd, Hewson and Baxter. At Wigan Pier they went by with a minute in hand over Neal, Ellison, Penvose, Taylor and Keenahan who were chasing grimly.

There was a bit of panic that the team cars would not get through to the feeding station because of a pile up of a petrol lorry with a small van in Warrington. Les Tanswell, the Transport Controller, turned on the heat and they sizzled past with about 4 miles to go. Luckily the bloke in charge of feeding had moved the feeding station up about 2 miles, so the panic just became a minor race against time.

Paddy Boyd was anxious to get to Queensferry to see his 'mum' and took his musette too quickly, got it tangled in his front wheel and kissed the ground! He had a further stop later on when his gear suddenly disintegrated into thin air, but a real storming 4 miles saw him back with the leading group, and he got a great cheer from the Army mob as he received second place in the Border *prime*.

An estimated 10,000 people saw the finish at Colwyn Bay, and I can quite believe it. There was a heat haze on the promenade and in the far distance a small cloud of dust was seen. It became bigger – riders moving like a rolling sea in line abreast. Just like the waves on the shore, first one moved forward, then another. The crowds went wild, urging on the sweating, sprinting riders. For the Judges to class them at inches was too much, for the whole 12 could be accommodated in the space of one bike length. Dickie Boyd got the verdict by a gnat's whisker from Hewson and Penvose, while the other howling dervishes were sorted out in their order.

$7\frac{1}{2}$ minutes later the pack came in and several old ladies nearly had heart failure as this giant mass of riders bore down upon them. (In confidence afterwards, 2 nice old dears told me that they wouldn't have missed it for anything!) And again, Robinson retained his hold on the *maillot jaune*.

STAGE 8. COLWYN BAY TO WOLVERHAMPTON 128 MILES.

I rubbed my eyes more than once to make certain that I was awake when I got down to the start. There in front of me was a trick cyclist, 12 feet high, parading up and down in front of the pier. Soon he was joined by Coco the Clown, miniature ponies and girls in sparkling costumes, and the motley crowd watching and waiting for the 'off' got slightly hilarious.

The P.R.O. of Quakers looked a bit down in the mouth, and enquiries elicited the fact that it had always been one of his ambitions to have a stage of the 'Circuit' started by having ELEPHANTS in front . . . I thought this a little odd, but said nothing – the sun was hot, and the P.R.O. was not wearing a hat!

It was said afterwards that my eyes nearly popped out of my head, but that's a fairy tale, or it could be an elephant's tail, for lo and behold over the brow of the hill appeared Victor George Humphrey sitting high on an elephant's nut (elephant boy fashion) and, behind his elephant, there were 3 more, all holding one another's rudders.

By the time numerous pictures had been taken and they moved through the crowd there was but 2½ minutes to go. They just loved their Quick Quakers out of a box, and took box and all. But they completely blocked the road. 'There are 2 minutes to go lads, just 2 minutes to go.'

'*Excuse me*, would you mind moving your elephants?' They have got them down to the start, the problem now was to turn 'em round. One rider was getting himself nicely squeezed up against a lamp-post, and I had visions that I should have to tell his mum that he'd been flattened by an elephant. How *can* you explain that a bike rider has been flattened by an elephant? 'Would you MIND moving your elephants?'

'Calling all riders. On your bikes lads. One minute to go, one minute to go.'

'HALF a minute to go lads, half a minute to . . . get the flipping elephant . . . HEY! . . . get that . . .' Oscar took it into his head that a sitdown might do him good, but luckily the keeper saw him and walloped him across the 'you know where'. 'Fifteen seconds to go, lads. Would you please mind moving that ELEPHANT.'

'10', a pause while an elephant trumpets, '5, 4, 3, 2, 1, GO' and, as the last word came out over the Tannoy, Oscar lumbered away and the whole colourful cavalcade of the 'Circuit' commenced to roll. Phew!

As the de-neutralising flag went down, so the *prime* flag went up and the race, uphill, was on, and the scramble up the 600 foot climb resulted in Evans taking the prize.

Nearing Bettws-y-coed, 18 year old Phil Ellison (Yorkshire) dropped out of the back and looked as though he'd had more than enough. We talked to him of lovely things and talked him back to the bunch and he went straight through the field, taking Carroll and Armitage with him! With the dreaded Penmachno resurfaced, all the gingerbread had been taken from the climb, and the only thing the riders had to worry about was the Cyclo van strewn all over the place – burnt out, conked out, and left to the tender mercies of cycle mechanics!

Ellison grinned all over his face as, with a 50 second lead he plunged over the top, followed by the faithful 2. They linked up and literally dropped down from the clouds, Bala bound. But this year there was a detour around Arenig Fawr to be reckoned with. A road across the open mountain-side – a gravel and rutted road. Victor George was espied doing a Tarzan although there was no sign of any elephants. There was quite a crop of punctures on this stretch and they included Penvose, Holliday and Bristow.

Stones could not have dropped faster into Bala, and at the start of the Berwyn Mountains the 3 were still plodding merrily on, and Carroll took the *prime* from Ellison and Armitage. They spread their wings from here on for their lead increased with every passing minute. Through Llangynog and Llanfyllin they pounded, border bound and Carroll took the *prime* from Armitage, while Phil Ellison looked dead tired.

Through the feeding station they trundled kept down to 10 m.p.h. by a mobile marshal, and the field crawled through 8 minutes later. Out on the Shrewsbury By-pass, Ellison it was who stepped up the revs and got out of his doldrums, and it was Carroll and Armitage who now hung on by their eye-lashes.

Nearing Harley Bank, Ellison tipped the wink and bade them a fond farewell, and our speedo read a steady 26 as we motored behind him. At Much Wenlock and Bridgnorth he was still going strong, and we wished him 'God speed' as we left him for the finish at Wolverhampton.

Into this blaze of colour swept the tiny figure of Ellison, alone in his glory, hero of the day, and of the race, and everyone, officials included, rose to him, 18 years old, 8st 4lb, so much before him, so much behind him!

It was over 2 minutes later, that Tweddell (Army) beat Armitage in the sprint for 2nd place, with Frank Carroll beaten into 4th position. The rest of the mob came in 9½ minutes later. Viva Ellison!

But Robbo still held the race leaders jumper.

STAGE 9. WOLVERHAMPTON TO LONDON (POLYTECHNIC STADIUM)
136 MILES.

Because of a misunderstanding we got to the line with only 30 seconds to go in this, the last stage. There had been many whispers overnight of last minute action, and we could only wait and see the outcome.

7 miles go by and Kennedy broke a pedal, and although the bunch speeded up, Kennedy got back to the bunch on a team-mate's machine. At Stourbridge, Dowell and Needham (B.U.C.U.) crept away and by Bromsgrove had been joined by Perks and Nicholson (North East). At Stratford on Avon, the bard would not have been pleased to see the chaos left behind, but they now had a lead of 2½ minutes on Bailes, Sanderson, Bartrop and Waterfield.

Needham soon needed 'em, and went the way of all weak flesh. The 6 joined forces and eat ground between Ettington and Banbury. Here, Des Robinson was 8 minutes down on his challengers, but they would have to double that amount to knock him off his perch.

At Aynho we were in constant communication with the organiser because of Television coverage. As we entered the feeding station cameras began to whirr, but the 6 appeared oblivious and ploughed on regardless. We watched the antics of the cameraman as he straddled the top of the car and waited for a loud bump but nothing happened.

Through Bicester to Thame, the pattern was the same, except that we lost Jimmy Saville who departed for Aylesbury, while we made on towards London. At Thame, we 'genned' the leaders up that they had a 6½ minute lead, and soon after they climbed up the snakey Chinnor Hill. Jimmy Saville was but a voice crying in the wilderness, 'Will someone please tell me where I am!'

At West Wycombe we briefed Vic, who was at Beaconsfield, on the situation, got some more 'gen' from Les Tanswell and learnt that the leaders now had 7½ minutes in hand, and that Jimmy had now been pin-pointed and had his car pointed in the right direction.

At Beaconsfield we picked up 'Mustachios' Glendinning, and the lead had become 8½ minutes. We gave them a jolt every now and again with the Tannoy, just to keep their minds on their work. At Northolt the lead had increased (to 9 minutes) and so had the volume of traffic. Dowell's chain suddenly did an almighty fandango and off he went from the back.

We hastened forward to the glare and glitter of the Polytechnic Stadium, where we just had time to park and scurried off to the finishing line before the first arrivals. As they entered the Stadium, there were still 5, with Sanderson first in and pounding his gears for dead life. On the cinder track he skidded and swayed, holding himself upright by sheer effort and he made it to the line in a series of jerks and sideway slips, followed by Bartrop, Perks and Bailes in that order.

9 minutes and 11 seconds later a huge group of 40 riders hurled themselves round the track and burst across the line, and the 1955 Circuit of Britain was virtually over.

There was the race dinner of course, which just had to be a success, for the menu was elaborate and the cross-toasting hilarious. Of course, if you wanted facts and figures, these could be supplied; it was Desmond Robinson of Yorkshire who won in 49.16.31, with Derek Evans (South Central) in 2nd spot at 1 minute 31 seconds, with Ray Holliday (R.A.F.), 3rd at 4 minutes 26 seconds. Yorkshire won the team race, and the mighty 'King of the Mountains' was that hill-climbing expert, Jock Kennedy of Scotland, with Brian Haskell of Yorkshire as the runner-up.

9: Over the 'Brown'

Circuit of Britain, 1956
August 11th—18th

The 3rd in the series of cycling dynamics was to take place in the 'summer' month of August, 1956, and August was a month in which some sunshine was to be expected, but the whole race was marred by the weather. Heavy winds, together with torrential rain, thinned the field down by crashes, etc., making the race appear ragged and inconsistent. There must be added to this the fact that the publicity experts had not really done their homework, and also the fact that Vic Humphrey had let the 'brown' run away with him.

So much so, in fact, that at one time there was talk of the riders going on strike! It will probably be thought by many that this was the roughest and toughest bike race ever in this country, and they might not be far wrong at that either!

Narrow roads, steep hills, fantastic gradients, everyone could understand, but the diabolical 'bits and pieces' that were included in the race were much too tough, and more reminiscent of a cyclo-cross event than a stage-race. There were those who said the riders were just riding to finish, not to win, while others said that it was a good race, that it was the organisation that was 'up the pole', but one thing stood out above all others, there was a 'flap' on every day, and the 'flaps' got bigger, brighter and better as the race progressed.

The race is booked to start on the 'wide open spaces' of the East Coast, at Skegness to be precise, and it was there that bike-riders; team managers; routeing teams; timekeepers; judges and all the other officials found their way. The wind moaned and

147

howled across the flat sea-bed, and Vic, as usual, laid down the law on what was to be what.

At this stage everything seemed to fall into place nicely. There was a bit of tension, there always is – jerseys, track-suits and the glittering bikes. There was the 'off-beat' gesture of a rider to an official that showed a display of nerves; gestures; grimaces; the last minute testing of gears by the Service men; the blowing up of tyres; the checking of machines and wheels; the revving up of engines and the clatter of shoe-plates – all went to create an atmosphere of a big race occasion.

But under all the banter and the sparkle there was something that was indefinable, perhaps a sparkle that was waiting to pounce and ignite. Perhaps just one's imagination, but there were many who left the briefing who were glad to be out in the air again.

6 donkeys huddled together on the small strip of sand by the Tower Esplanade and a cold, freak wind blew across the incoming tide. The bucket and spade and candy floss stalls were barred and shuttered and on the main street the lights still blaze on the Bingo Hall . . . a small chalked notice outside a cafe advertised 'Morning Coffee'.

The cold wind sent the riders scurrying for what shelter they can find before the 'off', and the dull cloudy conditions and dreary sea-mist did not help to raise their spirits. Finally, all was sorted out and the riders lined-up in serried, shivering ranks and it seemed a pity to spoil the pattern as they huddled together, but the Chairman of the Council finally lowered the 'Jack' and away they ambled for the race was neutralised out of the town.

STAGE 1.
SKEGNESS TO MANCHESTER 138 MILES THAT BECAME 163 MILES.

Such was the length of the stage that the routeing team had left at 5.0 a.m. and they reckoned they would just about beat us in. The 10.45 a.m. start was moved forward and we actually left at 10.30 and the rain had kept off.

They were moving well, with the wind dead behind, but *we* couldn't have been moving all that well for the level-crossing gates closed smack in our faces and the riders were on the other side. It was a hair-raising 10 miles before we caught them, and a break of six had gone, and the rain had caught up with us. Gradually it increased in ferocity until it was a torrential downpour and, to make it even worse, the course changed direction and they ran into a strong head-wind that was near to gale force. We missed McNeil (North East) as his back tyre blew and he went bumpety-bump along the road. Cyclo loomed up and the lad got a '100 yards start' as Johnny Morris pushed him off on the way back to the bunch.

We swept into Burwell and the break had a nice healthy looking lead on the *peloton,* which was now strung out like so much dirty washing on a line. So hard did the rain come down that it was virtually impossible to tell one colour from another. They splashed through giant puddles, sloshed round this and that bend, and always the wind howled at them.

A minute behind the leaders was a group led by Bill Bradley (Merseyside) and at a further half minute another bunch of twenty or so. In Louth, the country traffic was slow and dense, police reaction was not swift or sure. Traffic lights loomed up, and sundry odd bods jumped the lights, while others took to the pavement to save accidents. Police notebooks came out and numbers were taken, and the organiser was warned that there might be prosecutions for traffic infringements.

Victor blew his top and talked of giving out time penalties left, right and centre; by the time we got going again, the leaders had literally vanished. We belted the daylights out of the car and after 10 'Fangio' driven miles decided that something is radically wrong. It was . . . all the riders were *completely* off course!

With the high wind and the rain the routeing arrows had blown away (I wonder!). Officials were stopped, turned around and sent off to catch the main bunch dawdling along at Ludborough, while we had to go on as far as Holton le Clay before catching the leaders. We turned 'em round and chivvied them back to Elkington Cow Pasture, which some wag suggested was just about right, and could they please get on with the race, 'cos he was bloody wet!

We started 'em off, with the leaders at a discreet interval in front of the *peloton,* and the weather took it into its head to get worse. Once they got going we thought our troubles were over, but we had forgotten about the feeding wagon, and that was well and truly on its way to Grimsby. Luckily, many of the managers had food of sorts with them and a hasty feeding station was set up, everyone getting a little bit of something and, after what seemed hours and hours, we again saw the riders.

By this time it was well on in the afternoon, and at Rotherham (93 miles) we were 2 hours down on schedule, and things had been happening. Now there was no break, just gormless Norman Taylor bashing it out 400 yards in front of a huge bunch being led by Norton (Yorkshire). They were travelling at lightning speed, all of 15 m.p.h. and right behind, at 7 minutes, came Phil Ellison (Yorkshire).

On the stiff climb out of Rotherham, several chanced their arm and several groups formed and a 13 strong bunch soon had a 1½ minute lead. They roared down the 1 in 6 to Oughtibridge, through a herd of cows, and on to another stiff climb smack through Oughtibridge village to a HALT sign, bang in the middle. Like flies they clawed and crawled their way up the hill, with dirt, mud, sweat and anguish registering on their faces, and it was Bradley who took the *prime*.

Through narrow, winding lanes they dropped like shooting stars, and there was still 30 odd miles and more to cover. The light was beginning to fade now and so they plodded on, small bunches in two's and three's, keeping one another company, all tearing down and crawling up through wonderful scenery with many sheep adrift on the roads.

The lead now was left in the hands of Pete Ward (N.W.); Taylor (N.E.); Goddard (London); Norton (Yorks); Gil Taylor (Warwick); Rae (Scotland) and Bradley. Came the Snake Pass and Gil Taylor took wing and at the top had a lead of 3½ minutes. Ward had punctured in both legs, and Goddard was not breathing so good. Norton said he wanted to be sick!

Down, down, down they screamed, four chasing one, who was never to be out there long on his own. At Mottram, 9 miles from the finish they caught him, gave him a sailor's farewell, but he would not have it, and all 5 bashed on into the gathering dusk.

The race was scheduled to finish just before a Speedway meeting at the Belle Vue Stadium, but so late were we that *the meeting was over*, and we had the humiliation of finishing in an adjacent car-park. All 5 scrambled in together but it was Jimmy Rae who found the strength to push his wheel in front and beat McNeil and Norman Taylor. Time for the official 138 miles (later changed to 154, then 158, but registered on our speedo at *163 miles*) 8 hrs. 28 mins. 30 seconds.

As late-duty timekeeper and judge we waited, and waited and waited. One by one they came in and finally the pick-up team came in to say that there were still 5 lonely souls plodding their way towards Manchester, and it was nearly a quarter past 9 at night before our duty was done for the day.

A ride, *not a race,* that will surely be remembered by all who took part!

And what of the night? The Result Sheet bore an imposing list of penalties in time, and the directive that 'This race may well be the deciding factor for the future of Road Racing in this country. It is up to you all to set a high standard of riding.'

Luckily a sense of humour abounded, and there were tears of laughter on many of the riders faces as they struggled into Glossop and saw the huge sign in front of them *'It's a joy ride to Belle Vue'.*

STAGE 2. MANCHESTER TO MORECAMBE 131 MILES (PERHAPS).

It obviously wasn't going to be Vic's year! British riders had never experienced anything like this before, and a full 8 hour session on a bike would have been good enough for any professional at that time. As officials we didn't really know whether to laugh or cry, or to feel sorry for Vic and, to crown our misery, the start of the 2nd stage didn't help any.

We were right in the middle of Manchester at Whitworth Park and, although it was not raining yet, it was already threatening to do so. Some of yesterday's tail-enders were looking shattered already, and despite ribald comments bandied about amongst ourselves, no-one was all that cheerful.

The Chairman of the Parks Committee said a few words, helped put the yellow jersey on Rae, dropped the flag and another stage had started. Through the intricacies of Manchester roads we meandered – Higher Ardwick, Pin Mill Brow, Great Ancoats Street and on to the Rochdale Road. It was not clogs that made the clatter, but the juggling of gears as the neutralised period came to an end. The rain by this time was well and truly with us.

At Middleton Watson, Law, Crozier, Mather, McPherson, Ward, Nicholson, Bradley, Goss, Norton, Jackson, McNeil, Wright, Pinnington and Gil Taylor broke. Mile after mile of built-up area skimmed under their flying wheels, while the *peloton* rode itself stupid to get with them, but that was the break that was to supply the winner that day.

On through Bury, Ramsbottom and Rawtenstall they went, on a route which today would be impossible because of traffic conditions. But then it was the thing – crowds were out cheering, people watching from doorways and windows and all helping to make it a carnival occasion. At Sagarholme they had a 5 minute lead, and then, the day's fun begins.

A screamingly sharp left-hander through a wooden gate and the start of a climb, sheep-strewn in parts, grass-tufted in others. This was a prelude to mile after mile of similar roads (?), lanes and moorland tracks, and the riders, in the rain, did not appreciate it. They rattled over a cattle-grid, back wheels skidding in protest, and started a descent that sent cold shivers down the spine. Came another upward drag, straight into the teeth of the wind, another grid, and then down they shot into Burnley's midst at a horrific pace.

Back in the *peloton*, Rae was a laugh, and comedian that he was he shot off with Clements (Midlands) and Doug Collins (Army) in hot pursuit. He skilfully peeled a banana and heaved the skin well to the left, and no one was more astonished than the young lady in whose hat it fell. But the lead had now reached 5½ minutes.

The leaders pounded out the rhythm and the sun came out as a real blessing. By Colne they were really nicking well together, drying off in the sunshine and keeping up a terrific pace on the climb through Colne and on through Thornton in Craven.

Then came sudden sharp turns with stiff climbs, then on through narrow, walled-in, winding lanes they sped, the sun now hot and high as they screamed round bends, climbing twisting, dropping, turning, and still they hammered it out. Suddenly, *it was all happening*, as Jimmy Saville, our announcer commented.

We scared the daylights out of ourselves with a sharp right hand turn through a very narrow gate and we were on a grass-grown track *with not a road in sight*. Flints, boulders, dips and crevasses were all part of the fun, and this gave way to lush green, slippery grass. A grass-covered hill did not bother the riders, for they just jumped off their bikes and scrambled up and over.

Meanwhile – all hell was let loose. The leaders had gone long since, but a Police car, Press cars, the Cyclo van, one or two team and official cars were attacking this slippery obstruction in their path like a swarm of angry ants and, in the midst of all this, the *peloton* turned up. A red-faced Vic Humphrey stood by the side of his car apologising over the Tannoy, but the riders just did not want to know, they just wanted to get to the other side. A rider fell into a ditch and was helped out by a copper, and they looked at one another and laughed their heads off.

They all got over somehow and slithered down the rock-strewn atrocity only to find themselves wading through thick mud at the bottom of a deep hole. Oh, well! The leaders went this way and so we had to as well! Out on to a metalled road once more and, even with all the fun and games, the leaders had only a 5 minute lead.

There was a banging from underneath our car and investigation showed that we had picked up a giant rock from somewhere and it had jammed in, and just walloped the ground every time we hit a bump. We got rid of it somehow, and discovered that the petrol tank had a huge dent in it, but pressed on regardless!

It was at Malham that we caught up with the leaders, only 3 now in Bradley, Mather and Jackson. The rest were strung out like dirty linen on a line. They were to remain like this to the end, wending their way through twisting, fantastic lanes, with steep climbs followed by hair-raising descents over sheepish moorland roads. We slipped over bridges with only 2 to 3 inches to spare, and met a not-so-friendly G.P.O. van coming the other way. Luckily there was a gate handy and the 3 riders and us went in one gate and out the other, and at least we could breathe again.

Soon the narrow road opened into a vista of breathtaking beauty, and you could virtually hear the short intake of breath from the three fast-moving riders. A cloud nestled cosily on the head of the mountain and the grey ribbon of road moved lazily into the vast distance. Fantastic corners, many of them 1 in 6, reached up with hungry hands. Grit strewn corners, that could bring punctures in their wake. Water tinkled merrily from rock to rock as it made its way down to the valley left far behind.

The Darnbrook Fell *prime* went to Bill Bradley and it was worth its weight in gates for we have already gone through 6, before reaching the *prime* point at 'Telegraph Pole 48' through the seventh gate. We warned the riders of dangerous bends ahead, but it was us that needed the warning.

They dropped into the abyss like stones and along another narrow, rocky ledge of a road to Arncliffe. From here it was a doddle to Kettlewell and its river bridge, and I, for one, felt like diving straight into the cool looking water. Along the River Wharfe they scrambled to Buckden, while behind them the Ambulance was picking up some pieces when Corfield and Jimmy Mather got tangled up together on one of the descents.

They took the welcome food and drink at the feeding station, and had just enough time to stuff it into their pockets when a 1 in 5 sign told them that this was the Greenside *prime* (oh Vic, how could you?). Bill Bradley's tyre and gear cable gave out, and his breathing was not so good either, and it was Charlie Mather who got up first, followed by a running Peter Ward, and then Jackson.

It was Ward and Mather who got together on the long, long swoop down to Hawes, and they made hay while the sun shone, for behind them were 5 chasers in Gil Taylor, Bradley, McNeil, Jackson and McPherson. Gradually however, they pulled away and, as they commenced the climb (yes, another one!) of the Whernside Mountains they learnt that they had $5\frac{1}{2}$ minutes on the Bradley group and *14 minutes* on the *peloton,* and it was Ward who took the *prime.*

Down they hurtled towards Cowan Bridge, and Mather took a header over his handlebars on a corner. Nothing much, but he had pulled a muscle and though he got back with Ward, he was not the man he was. They took it in turns at the front, Pete Ward's getting longer and longer and, just after Carnforth, he left Mather and finished in front of thousands on the sea-front at Morecambe.

Charlie Mather limped in just over a minute later, with the Bradley group a further 5 minutes behind, and the rest, way back to John Holland (Army) at *2 hours and 4 minutes.* It was after

6.0 p.m. when Ward finished and it was getting dark when the exhausted Holland freewheeled in.

It had been a hard, hard day, and Peter Ward now headed the General Classification by 2¼ minutes from Bill Bradley, with Gil Taylor in 3rd spot, a minute away, and John Holland *at 4 hours and 17 seconds after only 2 days of riding!*

STAGE 3.   MORECAMBE TO RHYL   115 MILES.

There was quite a crop of bandaged limbs at the start, and many more were really sore where they sit down! Seats were provided but most of them preferred to stand, and one or two officials had matchsticks to keep their eyes open so little sleep did they get. Bill Bradley complained of pains in his knees, and did not look all that good.

Almost before we were out of town, Watson (Scotland) slithered to a halt with a puncture, but swift work by G.B. and he was back in the fold just after Lancaster. The thundering lorries were halted (no M.6 then!) while we left the main drag and Ward was up at the front as they tore through Conder Green. Pinnington, suffering from a damaged leg muscle from the day before, was dropped and Brian Wiltcher was off with gear trouble.

They hammered into the wind and, at Garstang, Nicholson, Seggar and Nev Crane were pounding away, doing bit and bit in perfect tune with one another and soon have a 200 yard lead. They gradually increased this and got up to a minute but just after Bamber Bridge the lead had dropped to 15 seconds and the writing was on the wall.

At Preston, Bradley had come out through the back, ashen-faced and with huge blobs of sweat on his brow. He was obviously in great pain, and we now learnt that the slight knee trouble of the day had now really turned sour on him. We left him and chased up to the leaders to find Nicholson gone and Clements, Jackson, Rae, McPherson, Bristow, Whitaker and Ryan in his place. At Walton they went through with a nice 5 minutes on a group of five and 10 minutes on a group of seven more, and Bradley was *over half an hour down.*

Groups came and went, and there was no pattern any more and as they plugged into the now strong wind, the *peloton* had split in

155

two with poor old yellow jersey, Pete Ward, heading the first at 300 yards from the second. Up to the feeding station and so strong was the wind that marshals were not needed to slow 'em down, and the front half had a 2½ minute lead on the second bit, with the yellow jersey doing most of the work at the front. But they were still headed by the leaders who had gone through over 5 minutes before.

The 9 hammered away for mile after mile, happy in the knowledge that the more they did now, the more they would be in front at the finish. At Flint, it happened again, and we turned sharp left, and shot into a grassy lane, which went up, and up, but UP!

Ryan and Clements did a little dance of joy and tried to leave the others behind and we learnt that Hutton, Saunders, McNeil and Purdy were doing their crust to get up with the leaders. Came a harsh moorland grind, sharp gritted, and Seggar departed, then Jackson, then Bristow and then McPherson in that order. They hurtled down towards Babell, aptly named in the circumstances, and Bristow and McPherson made it a tandem.

Crowds lined the streets in thick profusion in Holywell, and colourful 'stones' dropped from out of the blue to the place beneath, the main coast road. McPherson 'skipped' the corner and Bristow nearly got off to see if he had stopped and, at Mostyn, McPherson caught Ryan and Rae, but the elusive Clements was not there any more.

Frank had but a flimsy lead and the wind was making the going real tough. 3 against 1 were the odds, but he pressed on, bespattered and begrimed, sweat-streaked and dead weary. Purdy, Hutton, McNeil and Saunders had caught and dropped Jackson and Seggar and were now pounding on the heels of Bristow.

Into the wind Clements ploughed, not gaining and not losing anything, while Johnny Ryan took off a mile from the finish, and so it was Clements who took the stage, staggering drunkenly across the line, just 36 seconds in front of Ryan, who in turn was 1 minute, 13 seconds in front of McPherson and Rae. At 8 minutes past 7 in the evening, 8 hours and 8 minutes after leaving Morecambe, Bradley, Pinnington and Richardson limped in, and so bad was Bill Bradley's knee that he had to call it a day, and went back home.

Over the 'Brown'

PART ONE

This was a novel and new innovation for any 'Tour' of Britain –
a split stage. Novel was right, for although according to race
regulations, everybody will get a 30 minute break in Barmouth, it
was to be a nightmare of a stage that should have been thought
twice about.

They left the front at Rhyl dead on time, but by the time
Gwytherin was reached they were already 15 minutes down on
schedule. We turned sharp right and proceeded up past a school,
and then left over a goat track. It was a gated road of course.
Narrow, winding, with sharp corners, and the route went up, down
and around and soon split the field from here back to the
schoolhouse. Anguish was on most faces and one or two riders
were sick. The Merseyside team manager, riding on a motor-
scooter, missed a right-hander, did a little waltz up the road and
deposited the two thereon on to the ground, the manager getting a
badly grazed arm.

Cars continually stuck on corners, or at narrow gates, and there
was no room to pass; if a rider caught you, it was easier for
him to get off and run round when there was space. The press,
having missed the break, were fuming at the back 'cos they could
not get through, while right up at the front, Ron Killey (Mersey)
was wallowing in the rough going and took the Friddog *prime*.
Airey-fairy lanes followed and so far behind was Pinnington
(Wales) that he would just about have time to get home and back
before next year's race starts!

Eventually we came out on to a metalled road and little groups
got together and it was a joy to see more than one rider at a time.
Bodenham (Warks) went the way of all flesh. Ryan, Killey, Gil
Taylor, Charlie Mather, Ellison and Clements streamed in one
long line through the Vale of Penmachno and out on to the gated
road that led up to the Pen-y-Bedw *prime*. It was a grim struggle
and they crept like tiny coloured beetles up the face of the wall,
and Clements crashed and got slight concussion. Behind them,
Seggar walked with a broken chain (the Service vehicles hadn't got
through yet!), and Armstrong, F. Ward (London) and McPherson
were hammering in luke-warm pursuit of a large bunch that they
finally managed to catch just short of Harlech.

157

Cycling's 'Circus'

The 5 ugly sisters in Ryan, Clements, Taylor, Ellison and Mather were destined to stay away to the finish, although Clements certainly looked the worse for wear. On the sea-front the officials waited in the road marked off, and it was on the adjacent road that the 5 fought out the finish, with not one official in sight!

They told the organiser in a few choice words what they thought of his race, and the red-faced Vic promised to make up the prize values, and all 5 were declared equal first in the time of 3 hours 10 minutes. Sustenance in the form of anything available was crammed into mouths and washed down with water, tea, fruit juices and anything else that came to hand, and all too soon for most, it was time for the 2nd leg to Aberystwyth.

PART TWO

Off went the redoubtable 5, and 10 miles out there was an 11 mile detour that could easily, under the circumstances, have been cut out, to help the sponsor with his publicity at Aberystwyth, but it was not to be so.

Up, around, along and over another series of goat tracks, and the narrow twisting climb took its inevitable toll. Rider after rider suffered cramp. Rider after rider came off the back like a yo-yo. The sponsors' P.R.O. got stuck on a mound of earth and threatened to call the race 'The Goats'.

Down at Dolgelly (for the second time) riders were still coming up from Barmouth to commence their detour, while the leaders were climbing out of Dolgelly on their way to Aberystwyth. Down they hurtled like so many sacred rabbits to Machynlleth and the bunches changed their format with a rapidity that was not easily understood. In the late afternoon we had the riders stretched out over mile after mile of rugged Welsh countryside, and it would be laughable if indeed it wasn't such a fiasco.

At Talybont, it happened again. Another detour which, since we were so far down on schedule, could easily have been cut out, but no, on we went crossing bridges 1, 2, 3, 4, and after 7 miles we were back *exactly one mile* from where we started. Up in front was Killey, Bristow and Dick McNeil, and nearly 4 minutes behind them came Ryan, Collins and a ghastly faced Clements, with the rest up to a further hour down.

The leaders skidded sharply at the HALT sign on the A.44 and

158

THE CIRCUIT OF BRITAIN - 1956

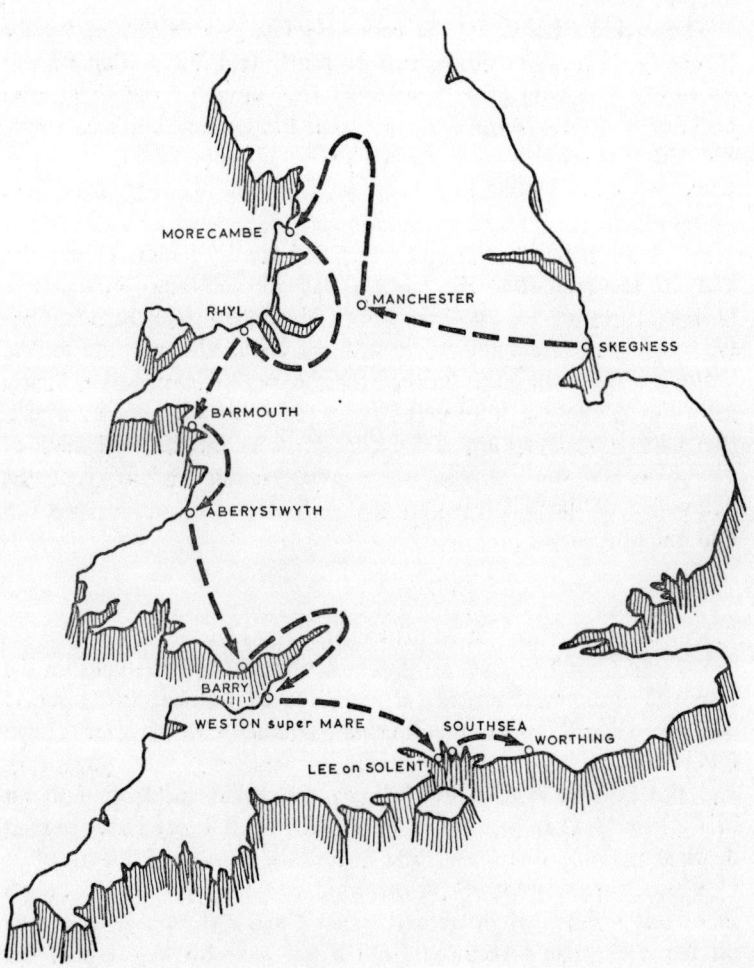

a solitary car did a fandango up the road as the occupants tried to see what was going on. Luckily, the level-crossing was open and all thankfully got across. They scrambled through Bridge Street and down to the Pier. A sharp left-hander put McNeil in the head, but a further left-hander came up quickly and Killey went by on the outside, Bristow could not get through on the inside and so, at nearly 8 minutes past 6 on a summer's evening, Killey (Mersey) won the stage by one second from Dick McNeil, with Bristow at another second.

The luckless holder of the yellow jersey, Rae of Scotland came in nearly 6½ minutes down, and promptly told Victor that he was no ruddy mountain goat. 6 unhappy lads were still out there after an hour had passed and we learnt that Pinnington didn't go round the Dolgelly circuit and got an extra 32 minutes on his time, while Norman Taylor had been *mis-directed* and had been sent round again!

All in all, it had been quite a day and finally, 1 hour 18 minutes and 10 seconds after the leaders had hit the line, Richardson, Stokoe, Norman Taylor (him what did another lap), Prince, Corfield and Bodenham limped in and we could all go home to tea.

But we were not quite finished for the day's Classification Sheets gave the interesting information, gleaned from who knows where, that Clements, Ryan and Gil Taylor were to get the equivalent of 1st prize for the 1st half stage and Mather and Ellison, the equivalent of the 3rd prize for that half stage . . . and I never did find out who sorted that out!

STAGE 5. ABERYSTWYTH TO BARRY   139 MILES.

We had 61 left to start on this, one of the toughest stages on the race and Cyclo were already at work before the neutralised period came to an end for Jimmy Rae had trouble with his gear. Gwyn Lewis and Jimmy Mather came out suddenly with punctures, and the bottom bracket of Roberts (Western) suddenly fell out into the road. G.B. just got started again when Terry Law stopped dead in front of them, and that meant the change of 2 wheels!

A small break went off on the wind-swept heights; in the bunch there was a flurry of riders and Brian Crozier (London) was lying on the deck, blood spurting from a cut near his eye. Up at the

Devil's Bridge they were pounding it out and it was every man for himself, to keep as many bods between him and the wind as they could.

In quick succession, Hall, Ellison, Prince, Corfield and Richardson were tailed off, and Mick Bingham (N.E.) led the bunch, but Bristow and Pinnington had already departed, Elan Valley *prime* bound. Through gates and along narrow roads carved out of the mountainside they hurry, and it was Pinnington, nearly last on General Classification, who took the *prime*.

Down, down into the desolate valley, over little bridges, flung like matchsticks across storming streams; through fiords, that were mere trickles, but on a rainy day would be torrents. On, on into the wild distance, where there was little sight of man, and the only beasts were the wild mountain sheep.

Along the valley they hurried, the brown waters swirled and snarled their way onwards. Again came a climb and the riders ground their way up, into the vastness stretching away. The trees had long since gone, and all we had to look at was road, and the greatness of the bare mountains, majestic, but foreboding in their vastness. The stillness was broken only by the whirr of the gears being changed, but on every rider the muscles stood out like whipcord as he battered his puny strength against the mountain.

They screamed down to thunderous applause in Rhayader, gaining on the bunch with every push of the pedals, but on the Upper Chapel *prime,* poor old Pinnington's bandaged knee began to go wonk again and it was Bristow who took it, while the 'Pin' dropped back to the shelter of the bunch.

Sheep stared at Bristow as he swept past and he did not care a 'baa' for them either. Through Coed-yr-ynys (it can't possibly be a name!) they hammered the dirt and Bristow thankfully came to rest in the bunch. On they hurried to the 3rd *prime* at Blaen Onneau and it was Nicholson who clambered up this stark mountain road to take the points.

Not a thing, a person, or a house in sight as they sped towards the feeding station and the colourful musettes stood out starkly against the blue sky. McNeil thankfully swung his on to his shoulder, hitched up his shorts and tucked in behind Nicholson. Together they reached the sky-line before Norman Taylor and the rest came through, but Bristow had had enough and went out through the back.

Down into the industrial area of Merthyr Tydfil they hurtled, picking up McNeil and Nicholson on the way and the 4th *prime* of the day came into sight, not at all welcome, as the rain began to fall. The road was a scar cut up, into and over the mountain, and McNeil took off and gained a minute at the top on the group, who were still turning 'em round, but wishing they were somewhere else.

They belted into Treherbert, and through Treorchy and on to Rhondda, and the pace was really hotting up. Pinnington punctured and, and by the time he got a wheel and was on his way, he was 2 minutes down. The leaders began to break up under pressure and Norman Taylor punctured in both legs. Saunders and Nicholson allowed daylight to creep in, and had to work themselves nearly to a standstill before making contact again.

Pinnington used every device known to bike-riders and with 14 miles to go he was back with the leaders. With only 9 miles left, a level-crossing gate closed suddenly and it was only after a parlez-vous with the gate-keeper that he became over-generous and let them through the side gate. Lucky Norm Taylor stormed up just as they open, and the rest were 6 minutes back and more.

Of the 6, it was Saunders who was sagging at the knees and with 8 miles left, he called it a day and waved the 5 'goodbye'. Back in the bunch, Charlie Mather, King of the Conks, bounced off a dog, visited a doctor who advised him to pack – got back on his bike, and finished the stage.

At least we were to be in Barry before the crowds went home that day, even although we were an hour down on schedule, and the five worked well together, like so many well-trained soldiers. As they burst on to the front, Pat Pinnington tried a long one, but brave lad that he was, it was not to be, for he was baulked by a spectator, and Clements, Gil Taylor and McNeil swept by in that order, leaving him with the 4th spot and Nicholson 5th. Saunders came in 2 minutes 23 seconds down, and then came the nightly wait for the rag-tail-and-bobtail.

Only 51 were to finish, with four in Jim Mather, and Lewis (Wales), Clark (South) and Harrison (Warwicks) 1 hour and 23 minutes behind the leaders, and poor old Charlie Mather crept in, having run into a dog, bandaged bound at 1 hour and 27½ minutes. Rag-tail-and-bobtail they might have been, but bloody heroes every one!

STAGE 6. BARRY TO WESTON SUPER MARE 132 MILES.

Too late it seemed, Vic decided that in view of the toughness of the course, and the near-gale-force winds delaying the riders' arrival at finishes, 10 miles were to be cut out of this stage. Every team had had trouble of some kind – Scotland had lost 2 men, while Yorkshire were down to one, and the only full team left in came from the South Eastern Counties.

Straight as an arrow they made for Gloucester with the wind, for the first time, dead behind. They literally screamed along, and 10 got away just beyond Cardiff but by Newport they were all one big happy family. After 30 miles they were at it again and Boyd, Saunders, Collins, Roberts, Nicholson, Clark, and Norm Taylor were grinding it out, and chasing like mad were the crazy 5 in Seggar, Smith, Bristow, Killey and Walter Shepherd (N.E.) Down the hill they pounded into Chepstow and Killey took a header over the top, crashing heavily.

He jumped up and scrambled after the leaders, blood flowing out and behind. He went at the *prime* hill like a mad thing, and swept past the others as though they had stopped. Up to Gloucester they went like an express train and, as they turned for the West Coast, the wind hit them and the pelting rain did not help.

Charlie Mather looked like a ghost riding along and he was obviously completely spent, and it was not long before he called it a day. At the feeding station the flying five were 5 minutes up on the yellow jersey, and no one wanted a drink, they were getting all they wanted from the rain!

They slithered through the traffic of Bristol and more than one official and copper got a few more grey hairs! Out on the other side, Killey took another toss, angrily scrambled back on his bike and got back to the other four. Paddy 'Dickie' Boyd and Clements were in pursuit and seemed to be gaining slowly. Up came Dundry Beacon and the picture changed again.

Walter Shepherd and Killey hared off and soon had 5 minutes on the others and into the narrow lanes they trundled at speed, being lost from sight for minutes on end as the lane twisted, turned and nearly did a rightabout on itself. Through Butcombe, Blagdon and Axbridge they hammered with Smith (S.E.) never very far behind. Brian Wiltcher was a couple of minutes back, while Clements, Boyd and Pinnington were a further minute behind him.

At Loxton, they turned into narrow, muddy lanes once more and, at Bleadon, there were only 3 miles to go. The surface was atrocious, and on a right-hander over they both went. Grazed arms, legs and a busted bike did not help any, but luckily the Cyclo van was handy and a spare machine was soon provided for the luckless Killey.

Shepherd went on as they were getting Killey put together in one piece again, and it was now Smith who did the chasing, with the blood dripping – Killey at a grey-faced distance behind. On to the Promenade, with hardly a soul in sight they made their way, and it was Shepherd who got the verdict from Smith, while Killey took a well-deserved 3rd. So sore and hurt was he that it took 2 stalwart men all their time to lift him off his bike.

Others ambled in in one's and two's, with sometimes, by way of a change, as many as 4 all together, herded as though for company. We lost 5 during the day, but Richardson, Lanterne, Rouge on General Classification managed to make it once again, 1 hour 43 minutes and 30 seconds after Shepherd.

STAGE 7. WESTON SUPER MARE TO LEE-ON-SOLENT 129 MILES.

Gil Taylor had taken over the red jersey for the 'King of the Mountains', and McNeil still had $14\frac{1}{2}$ minutes on him for the leaders doubloon. There was a sun of a kind as the Mayor of Weston dropped the flag, and I picked it up politely!

Outside the town, Birchall (Teesside), Mather, and Smith (S.E.) were fast fighting a losing battle off the back, and looked as though they were already in need of a tow rope. Road repairs, traffic lights, and BIG holes, not too well filled in, caused a bit of havoc and G.B. and Cyclo had a rare old time changing wheels, and there was now some light rain!

By Winscombe, the field was well spread out, and racing capes are flapping around in the stiff breeze. Cheddar Gorge looked chilly and uninviting but it had to be climbed, so down to work lads, and up we went. The rain seemed to have kept the cars away and they scrambled up through the grey rocks, not so much as an entity but as a chain that was stretched out. Banana salesman Johnny Ryan took the *prime*, and with the bit between his teeth did a death-defying drop down to Draycott.

So fast did he hammer that the chasers had to take chances and around Wookey Hole, old yellow jersey McNeil came a real purler, somersaulting over and over into a ditch. His leg was badly cut from thigh to ankle, and both wheels and gear damaged beyond repair, but the Cyclo Service vehicle was there once more, and soon Dick was on his way, aided and abetted by all and sundry, and within a few miles up came Cyclo and Dick changed back to his own machine.

Meanwhile, G.B. too were having fun for Doug. Collin's freewheel suddenly started going both ways at once and he found that he was pedalling like mad without moving an inch. As we approached Shepton Mallet we espied Boyd and Wiltcher ambling back the way we had come and enquiries elicited the fact that, having missed Collins they were on their way back to look for him. *How about that then!*

In Shepton, McNeil was in trouble again. Having got back on his own bike the bunch had moved on, and Dick, in his haste to get back to the shelter of the mob, had eyes only for them. A copper waved them through the traffic lights and then put up his mitt for McNeil to stop. Did he, heck! He and team-mate Ray Nye shot across this intersection on red, like bats out of hell, and out came the notebook and numbers were taken. The Chief Judge was there and managed to square things, and they copped an official, and unhealthy for them, 4 minutes penalty.

In a couple of miles, Nicholson's elastic broke, his legs turned to water, and he was off the back, and lost nearly ¾ hour between here and the finish. Down a 1 in 7 they hurtled and on to the market town of Frome. 5 had already climbed the hill to all points west and were being chased now by 4 more; at the feeding station the 5 went through with 3 minutes in hand, and the 4 chasers had nearly 7 minutes on the main *peloton*, including the yellow jersey.

The sun was out and felt hot to the skin and everyone suddenly wanted water. At Romsey, Dick McNeil was sweating it out at the front of the bunch and no-one wanted to take the lead. They dithered and dallied, dallied and dithered and the break got even further away. Dick's damaged leg looked rough, very rough indeed, but some of the motley crew in the *peloton* looked even rougher!

10 miles from the finish and the 5 in Seggar, Jackson, Shepherd, McPherson and Jim Grieves were moving like shots from a gun, with the chasing 4 at 4 minutes. Just as suddenly it slowed and within minutes we learnt that the chasers were only $2\frac{1}{2}$ minutes behind. Something clicked in what they called brains and Grieves went like a bullet from the back, and the others must have sensed that the timing was wrong, because they pulled him back.

At Titchfield, there were only 4 miles left, and on a slight rise, Jackson took flight, but the other 4 moved up and clipped his wings. Gears clanged as changes were made – riders sat watchful as yard followed yard and no-one made a move. Grieves pulled out all the stops with only 2 miles left, an exhausting chase by the others pulled him back, and there was but 1 mile to go.

Toe-straps were tightened as the yellow flag came into sight, and they jockeyed for position like so many ballerinas on a stage, and then *it was all happening*, for Shepherd took off and nearly took a kerbstone with him. Seggar took the middle line with Grieves on the outside. Jackson got up there and was headed by McPherson, Yardage was pounded away in a colourful streak and it was Jimmy Grieves (Warwicks) who got the win by a streak of light from Bill Seggar (S.E.) with the rest trailing at inches.

Most of the official vehicles used the floating bridge at Gosport while duty judge and timekeeper waited and waited and waited, and it was 2 hours and 37 minutes later that Birchall, Mather and Smith crawled in. The light was fading fast, and the officials just made it to their hotel for the evening meal. Throughout the whole of the race, if a 15% time limit had been imposed as had been suggested, we would have been down to 36 riders, and not the 46 we had at the present time.

STAGE 8.   SOUTHSEA TO WORTHING   85 MILES.
PART 1 – 34 MILES – CONTRE LE MONTE – COSHAM TO MIDHURST

With a 4 minute penalty, McNeil was a very, very thoughtful

lad at the start of the time-trial; he knew it would be a real test and, to add to his and everyone else's misery, there was a gale-force cross-wind. His leg, cut from his calf well up into his upper thigh, looked red raw and terribly sore.

The undulating course was a real 'testers' effort, and one by struggling one they took off from the Hilsea Lido at Cosham and climbed the hill on their way to the finish rendezvous. Pat Pinnington starting half-way down the field was in dead trouble and 20 riders passed him on the way and he clocked in the last of the 45.

In the meantime, Doug Collins had found the rhythm just right for him and beat out a splendid 1 hour 13 minutes 21 seconds to beat Ryan by 19 seconds, with Peter Dark a further 8 seconds away. Lunch was served and Dick McNeil looked a worried man, because his nearest rival, Gil Taylor had taken another 2 minutes out of him in the morning's 'trial', and his large lead of the day before had now been whittled back to $5\frac{1}{2}$ minutes.

PART 2 – MIDHURST TO WORTHING – ROAD RACE – 51 MILES

As they climbed up through the leafy lanes around Midhurst, all thoughts were on the fact that, only 50 odd miles away there was the finish, and they could get off their bikes for good and all. Crane (Yorkshire) got dropped in the same breath, and his laboured breathing could be heard for a very long way back.

Pat Pinnington too was suffering and his 2 damaged knees must be giving him agony. He made a faulty change and his chain flew off, and that was that! He sunk painfully to the ground at the side of the road, reached down and underwent toestrap, climbed to his feet gingerly, and proceeded to take all the hurt and the rage of the past few days out of his bike. It went up in the air and was slammed to the ground, again, again and again. Then he sank to his knees in supplication and cried the cry of the damned.

Johnny Morris, Cyclo, had been watching all this from just behind, and he leaped from the van and slapped Pinnington hard across the face. He pulled him to his feet and ordered him back on the bike. Having got him mounted he ran him along the road until suddenly he was earth-bound and took off after the *peloton* as though Morris and all hell was after him.

He rode like a lunatic, taking chance after chance; picking up Nev Crane on the way, they tandemed like merry hell and caught the bunch at Fittleworth. Gradually the field broke up, and the puncture fiend took its toll, and then the rains came. As they reached the last *prime* of the race, Johnny Ryan went off up Bury Hill on his own, but Nev Crane went after him together with Clements, but Ryan took it.

Everywhere you look there were riders banging away, forming little groups that became big groups, that disintegrated and became riders bombing away and the process went on over and over again. The whole bunch shot into Amberley and into a herd of cows. Hell reigned supreme for a few minutes, then all got through safely, but at Storrington, the whole were split into two, and the first bunch had built up a tidy lead.

Once again, we had a goat-track bit with only 13 miles to go, and as they turned off and climbed up a pimple of 1 in 6, a group of 6 got tangled up together and Dick McNeil was in the middle of it. Sportingly they sorted things out and put Dick back on his machine before remounting themselves, and they commenced to mow their way forward, picking up remnants as they went along.

Up at the front, the turmoil and the shouting had died, and a serious note crept into the proceedings. Doug Collins was roaring his way towards the finishing line, unheralded and unsung, while the others of his ilk and team were sitting comfortably on all and sundry, with them wondering what the devil it was all about. (It wasn't until the stage was over that anyone realised that when the herd of cows appeared at Amberley Collins had gone off, and Boyd and Wiltcher spotting this, sat on everything and everyone!)

Meanwhile, Pat Pinnington was off the back again, but struggled gamely on, with agony and anguish in every line of his face. The closing miles were covered in glory, because Collins had arrived on the West Parade, Worthing, 4 minutes ahead of anyone else, and all that was left were the crumbs from his plate and these went to team-mate Wiltcher, with Paddy Boyd, 3rd.

Gil Taylor had not had the strength or the inclination to do a flyer over the last 50 miles was still in 2nd place to McNeil, and was 3rd on the 'King of the Mountains' which, incidentally, went to Jim Nicholson (Tees-side), while the North Eastern Counties took the team race by over an hour from the Army C.U.

So Dick McNeil, 38th in 1955, won the last of the 'Oats' Circuits of Britain. It was announced at the Banquet that every finisher would get a bonus award of 2 pounds, perhaps to still conscience, perhaps as a tribute to those that did finish. It was, undoubtedly, the toughest stage race ever to have been perpetrated in this country, and one that certainly brought a lot of adverse publicity.

Without doubt, some of it would have been avoided, some of it was sheer bad luck, some of it man-made, and some of it, like the weather, in the lap of the gods but, whatever caused it, the event was never to be run again.

Tour of Britain 1951

RACE RESULTS

GENERAL CLASSIFICATION

Position	Name	Time
1	I. Steel – Viking	63.09.53
2	A. Taylor – Gnutti	63.16.09
3	I. Greenfield – Scotland	63.21.59
4	B. Wood – Pennine	63.32.31
5	J. Welch – Viking	63.35.00
6	K. Jowett – I.T.P.	63.36.34
7	E. Pierre – France	63.38.09
8	G. Audemard – France	63.44.07
9	K. McCarthy – Ireland	63.56.44
10	E. Garnier – France	63.57.32
11	E. Jones – Viking	63.59.05
12	F. Seel – I.T.P.	64.07.01

TEAM CLASSIFICATION

Position	Team	Time
1	Viking ..	190.08.13
2	France ..	190.48.30
3	I.T.P. ..	191.55.30

BEST AMATEUR

North London ..	195.21.53

FACTS AND FIGURES	Total prize value £850 Total distance 1,403 miles Race average m.p.h. 22.22 33 finished

KING OF THE MOUNTAINS
6 PRIMES

1	D. Bedwell .. .. (Withdrawn Stage 12)	11 points
2	K. Russell	6 points
3	A. Laurent	5 points
	I. Steel	5 points
5	J. Welch	4 points
6	F. Seel	2 points

STAGE RESULTS

Stage	Date	Route	Winner	Miles	Time
1	Aug. 19th	London – Brighton	G. Audemard	83	3.57.52
2	Aug. 20th	Brighton – Bournemouth	D. Bedwell	95	4.08.17
3	Aug. 21st	Bournemouth – Plymouth	I. Steel	122	5.40.06
4	Aug. 22nd	Plymouth – Weston-S-Mare	D. Bedwell	103	4.19.19
	Aug. 23rd	Rest Day			
5	Aug. 24th	Cardiff – Wolverhampton	K. Russell	112	5.22.17
6	Aug. 25th	Wolverhampton – Morecambe	I. Steel	127	5.07.40
7	Aug. 26th	Morecambe – Glasgow	I. Steel	160	6.22.32
8	Aug. 27th	Glasgow – Newcastle	D. Bedwell	150	6.46.02
9	Aug. 28th	Newcastle – Scarborough	D. Bedwell	88	4.16.05
	Aug. 29th	Rest Day			
10	Aug. 30th	Scarborough – Nottingham	L. West	125	5.28.25
11	Aug. 31st	Nottingham – Norwich	A. Laurent	123	5.43.55
12	Sept. 1st	Norwich – London (Hampstead Heath)	E. Garnier	115	5.29.41

Tour of Britain 1952

RACE RESULTS

GENERAL CLASSIFICATION

Position	Name	Time
1	K. Russell – Ellis-Briggs	61.26.49
2	L. Scales – Sun	61.29.49
3	R. Maitland – B.S.A.	61.31.29
4	I. Greenfield – Sun	61.39.08
5	I. Steel – Viking	61.39.40
6	G. Thomas – B.S.A.	61.43.58
7	B. Wood – Pennine	61.44.58
8	M. Michaux – Belgium	61.50.00
9	D. Robinson – Romford	61.50.30
10	W. Cook - R.A.F.	61.52.34
11	G. van den Dooren – Belgium	61.53.24
12	P. Proctor – B.S.A.	61.53.36

TEAM CLASSIFICATION

Position	Team	Time
1	B.S.A. ..	184.45.42
2	Viking ..	185.12.37
3	Pennine ..	185.18.31
4	Belgium ..	185.22.33
5	Romford ..	185.27.28
6	Sun ..	185.52.24

FACT AND FIGURES	Total prize value £1,013 Total distance 1,476½ miles Race average m.p.h. 23.97 43 finished

RACE RESULTS

KING OF THE MOUNTAINS 10 PRIMES			
1	P. Proctor	.. ..	19 points
2	I. Greenfield	.. ..	17 points
3	D. Clarke	.. ..	13 points
4	G. van den Dooren	..	10 points
5	R. Maitland	.. ..	9 points
	L. West	.. ..	9 points

STAGE RESULTS

Stage	Date	Route	Winner	Miles	Time
1	Aug. 22nd	Hastings – Southsea	J. Brackstone	99	4.12.27
2	Aug. 23rd	Southsea – Weymouth	K. Russell	85½	3.38.48
3	Aug. 24th	Weymouth – Weston-S-Mare	A. S. Jones	74	3.14.35
4	Aug. 25th	Cardiff – Aberystwyth	G. Gregorini	109½	5.01.53
5	Aug. 26th	Aberystwyth – Blackpool	K. Russell	179	7.58.37
	Aug. 27th	Rest Day			
6	Aug. 28th	Blackpool – Carlisle	L. Scales	90	3.36.35
7	Aug. 29th	Carlisle – Glasgow	G. van den Dooren	96	3.58.19
8	Aug. 30th	Glasgow – Dundee	L. Scales	85	3.11.29
9	Aug. 31st	Dundee – Edinburgh	I. Steel	91½	3.59.33
10	Sept. 1st	Edinburgh – Newcastle	L. Scales	112	4.32.27
11	Sept. 2nd	Newcastle – Scarborough	K. Russell	88	3.12.45
	Sept. 3rd	Rest Day			
12	Sept. 4th	Scarborough – Nottingham	T. Fenwick	125	4.38.03
13	Sept. 5th	Nottingham – Norwich	G. Thomas	123	4.04.28
14	Sept. 6th	Norwich – London (Alexandra Palace)	L. Scales	119	4.53.27

Tour of Britain 1953

RACE RESULTS

GENERAL CLASSIFICATION

Position	Name	Time
1	G. Thomas – B.S.A.	70.03.34
2	L. Scales – Wearwell	70.08.13
3	J. Pottier – Wearwell	70.09.55
4	B. Robinson – Ellis-Briggs	70.10.32
5	C. Parker – Hercules	70.12.00
	R. Maitland – B.S.A.	70.12.00
7	H. Guldemont – Belgium	70.13.55
8	M. Baele – France	70.14.48
9	B. Monti – Italy	70.15.53
10	L. Wilson – Pennine	70.20.13
11	R. Holliday – As. Eng. A	70.20.35
12	D. Bedwell – Hercules	70.24.17

TEAM CLASSIFICATION

Position	Team	Time
1	Wearwell ..	210.28.12
2	B.S.A. ..	210.53.15
3	Hercules ..	210.58.04
4	France ..	211.09.51
5	Belgium ..	211.14.19
6	Viking ..	211.24.31

FACTS AND FIGURES	
Total prize value £1,015	
Total distance	1,631 miles.
Race average m.p.h	23.30
42 finished	

KING OF THE MOUNTAINS 9 PRIMES			
1	D. Bedwell	.. ..	24 points
2	M. Baele	.. ..	14 points
3	A. Ilsley	.. ..	12 points
4	I. Greenfield	.. ..	11 points
5	G. Thomas	.. ..	8 points
6	D. Clarke	.. ..	7 points
	L. Wilson	.. ..	7 points

STAGE RESULTS

Stage	Date	Route	Winner	Miles	Time
1	Sept. 6th	London – Great Yarmouth	B. Monti	126	5.12.28
2	Sept. 7th	Yarmouth – Peterborough	L. Ciancola	102	4.03.10
		Peterborough – Leicester TT	H. Guldemont	40	1.37.20
3	Sept. 8th	Leicester – Leeds	M. Baele	134	5.54.15
4	Sept. 9th	Leeds – Scarborough	C. Parker	104	4.01.05
	Sept. 10th	Rest Day			
5	Sept. 11th	Scarborough – Newcastle	D. Bedwell	136	6.28.07
6	Sept. 12th	Newcastle – Glasgow	H. Guldemont	151½	6.49.17
7	Sept. 13th	Glasgow – Morecambe	D. Bedwell	164	7.06.56
8	Sept. 14th	Morecambe – Llandudno	C. Parker	125	5.19.44
	Sept. 15th	Rest Day			
9	Sept. 16th	Llandudno – Cheltenham	D. Bedwell	160	6.53.08
10	Sept. 17th	Cheltenham – Torquay	L. Chiti	152	6.53.52
11	Sept. 18th	Torquay – Bournemouth	G. Thomas	115	4.35.56
12	Sept. 19th	Bournemouth – London (Wembley – Olympic Way)	R. Grondalaers	121½	4.28.39

Tour of Britain 1954

RACE RESULTS

GENERAL CLASSIFICATION

Position	Name	Time
1	E. Tamburlini – France	60.12.15
2	B. Robinson – Ellis-Briggs	60.16.39
3	D. Bedwell – Hercules	60.20.36
4	J. Christison – Viking	60.21.14
5	G. Mercier – France	60.21.58
6	C. Parker – Hercules	60.22.21
7	I. Greenfield – Wearwell	60.23.17
8	D. Talbot – Hercules	60.23.51
9	I. Steel – Viking	60.24.10
10	R. Maitland – B.S.A.	60.26.10
11	F. Krebs – Hercules	60.26.30
12	A. Allamic – France	60.28.21

TEAM CLASSIFICATION

Position	Team	Time
1	France ..	180.56.49
2	Hercules ..	181.01.26
3	Wearwell ..	181.07.56
4	Viking ..	181.17.47
5	B.S.A. ..	181.19.12
6	Belgium ..	181.48.09
7	E. Briggs ..	181.48.36
8	Gnutti ..	183.43.26

FACTS AND FIGURES	Total prize value £1,506 Total distance 1,450½ miles Race average m.p.h. 24.10 39 finished

KING OF THE MOUNTAINS
8 PRIMES

1	H. Guldemont	..	17 points
2	B. Robinson ..	..	14 points
3	A. Newman ..	..	13 points
4	E. Tamburlini	..	12 points
5	D. Bedwell ..	..	11 points
6	I. Greenfield ..	..	10 points

STAGE RESULTS

Stage	Date	Route	Winner	Miles	Time
1	June 6th	Great Yarmouth – Lincoln	G. Mercier	128	4.53.11
2	June 7th	Lincoln – Manchester	F. Krebs	90	4.07.51
3	June 8th	Manchester – Harrogate	G. Mercier	75	2.52.01
4	June 9th	Harrogate – Whitley Bay	D. Bedwell	113	4.28.05
5	June 10th	Whitley Bay – Glasgow	D. Talbot	158	6.57.08
	June 11th	Rest Day			
6	June 12th	Glasgow – Morecambe	I. Greenfield	167	6.52.30
7	June 13th	Morecambe – Prestatyn	I. Greenfield	106	4.06.25
8	June 14th	Prestatyn – Llandudno TT	E. Tamburlini	42	1.50.42
9	June 15th	Llandudno – Wolverhampton	D. Bedwell	116	4.59.14
10	June 16th	Wolverhampton – Weston-S-M	D. Bedwell	129	5.42.55
11	June 17th	Weston-S-Mare – Torquay	I. Greenfield	91	3.45.57
12	June 18th	Torquay – Bournemouth	C. Parker	115	4.34.40
13	June 19th	Bournemouth – London (Alexandra Palace)	D. Bedwell	120½	4.52.23

173

Tour of Britain 1955

RACE RESULTS

GENERAL CLASSIFICATION

Position	Name	Time
1	A. Hewson – Sheffield	42.10.08
2	K. Mitchell – Wearwell	42.11.21
3	R. Bartrop – Sheffield	42.13.35
4	H. Guldemont – Belgium	42.14.35
5	J. Christison – Viking	42.15.25
6	I. Steel – Viking	42.15.42
7	J. Andrews – London	42.16.39
8	K. Russell – Rus/Wilson	42.17.30
9	D. Booker – Viking	42.18.14
10	J. Morris – London	42.19.33
11	D. Robinson – Leaguer	42.20.42
12	B. Pusey – Hercules	42.21.03

TEAM CLASSIFICATION

Position	Team	Time
1	Viking ..	126.26.52
2	Wearwell ..	126.59.32
3	Hercules ..	126.59.37
4	Internat. ..	127.04.39
5	London ..	127.12.23
6	Sheffield ..	127.28.34

FACTS AND FIGURES

Total prize value £1,000
Total distance 983 miles
Race average m.p.h. 23.30
34 finished

KING OF THE MOUNTAINS 9 PRIMES				
1	J. Forneau	..	..	28 points
2	B. Haskell	..	..	20 points
3	K. Mitchell	..	..	17 points
4	J. Andrews	..	..	14 points
5	T. Hewson	..	..	9 points

STAGE RESULTS

Stage	Date	Route	Winner	Miles	Time
1	Sept. 3rd	London – Clacton	J. Christison	74	2.52.13
2	Sept. 4th	Clacton – Skegness	R. Bartrop	152	6.17.09
3	Sept. 5th	Skegness – N. Holland	J. Andrews	73	2.54.26
		Hull – Filey TT	J. Christison	37	1.28.25
4	Sept. 6th	Filey – Sheffield	A. Hoar	95	3.57.44
5	Sept. 7th	Sheffield – Pwllheli	J. Mattivi	168	7.28.03
6	Sept. 8th	Pwllheli – Cheltenham	H. Guldemont	162	7.32.54
7	Sept. 9th	Cheltenham – Bournemouth	L. Scales	104	4.29.29
8	Sept. 10th	Bournemouth – London (Hampstead Heath)	D. Booker	118	4.44.53

Circuit of Britain 1954

RACE RESULTS

GENERAL CLASSIFICATION

Position	Name	Time
1	V. Bailes – Tees-side	44.55.50
2	D. Evans – Midlands	44.59.28
3	B. Haskell – Yorkshire	45.00.10
4	W. Armes – Tees-side	45.04.17
5	V. Stark – Essex	45.08.47
6	R. Godbeer – Essex	45.09.47
7	R. Mackin – North Eastern	45.12.32
8	F. Garvey – Manchester V.	45.12.58
9	T. Hewson – North Midlands	45.12.59
10	A. Keenahan – Tame Valley	45.16.28
11	W. Hodgson – Lakeland	45.17.52
12	I. Turner – South Midlands	45.18.18

TEAM CLASSIFICATION

Position	Team	Time
1	Lakeland ..	136.27.27
2	Tees-side ..	136.30.24
3	Midlands ..	136.45.51
4	North East	136.50.34
5	South Midlands..	137.04.41
6	Essex ..	137.31.13

FACTS AND FIGURES	Total prize value £632 Total distance 997 miles Race average m.p.h. 22.212 52 finished

KING OF THE MOUNTAINS 15 PRIMES	1	D. Lee ..	..	..	42 points
	2	T. Hewson	..	..	37 points
	3	B. Haskell	..	..	36 points
	4	R. Mackin	..	..	27 points
	5	B. Coombes ..	..	..	20 points
	6	T. Hadlington		..	16 points

STAGE RESULTS

Stage	Date	Route	Winner	Miles	Time
1	Aug. 14th	London – Nottingham	J. Kennedy	137	5.24.15
2	Aug. 15th	Nottingham – Scarborough	E. Duffy	121	5.27. 9
3	Aug. 16th	Scarborough – Morecambe	V. Stark	136	6.07.07
4	Aug. 17th	Morecambe – Rhyl	T. Hewson	118	5.15.29
5	Aug. 18th	Rhyl – Aberystwyth	D. Evans	105	4.54.32
6	Aug. 19th	Aberystwyth – Cheltenham	B. Coombes	130	5.46.45
7	Aug. 20th	Cheltenham – Weston-S-Mare	D. Harbottle	101	4.44.29
8	Aug. 21st	Weston-S-Mare – London (Southall)	L. Manns	149	6.53.30

175

Circuit of Britain 1955

RACE RESULTS

GENERAL CLASSIFICATION

Position	Name	Time
1	D. Robinson – Yorkshire	49.16.31
2	D. Evans – South Central	49.18.02
3	R. Holliday – R.A.F.	49.20.57
4	J. Kennedy – Scotland	49.23.09
5	R. Browne – Manchester	49.25.19
6	P. Ward – North West	49.26.30
7	E. Penvose – Yorkshire	49.28.48
8	P. Ellison – Yorkshire	49.33.31
9	B. Haskell – Yorkshire	49.35.10
10	M. Dowling – South West	49.36.00
11	A. Hewson – North Central	49.37.05
12	P. Boyd – Army C.U.	49.38.50

TEAM CLASSIFICATION

Position	Team	Time
1	Yorkshire ..	148.17.50
2	Manchester	149.02.39
3	Army C.U.	149.16.42
4	South Central ..	149.35.04
5	North East	150.11.40
6	North Central ..	150.29.35

FACTS AND FIGURES	Total prize value £463 Total distance 1,066 miles Race average m.p.h. 21.574 57 finished

KING OF THE MOUNTAINS 12 PRIMES	1	J. Kennedy	..	..	42 points
	2	B. Haskell	..	..	26 points
	3	F. Carroll	..	..	22 points
	4	D. Evans	..	..	18 points
	5	P. Boyd	..	..	17 points
	6	R. Browne	..	..	15 points

STAGE RESULTS

Stage	Date	Route	Winner	Miles	Time
1	July 15th	Manchester – Scarborough	J. Kenneday	147	7.01.48
2	July 16th	Scarborough – Whitley Bay	K. Stratford	112	5.01.45
3	July 17th	Whitley Bay – Musselburgh	R. Holliday	133	6.27.23
4	July 18th	Edinburgh – Glasgow	D. Robinson	57	2.14.08
5	July 19th	Glasgow – Carlisle	J. Perks	120	4.49.55
6	July 20th	Carlisle –Keswick TT	A. Jackson	36	1.33.07
		Keswick – Morecambe	D. Robinson	82	4.02.34
7	July 21st	Morecambe – Colwyn Bay	P. Boyd	117	5.12.08
8	July 22nd	Colwyn Bay – Wolverhampton	P. Ellison	128	6.05.26
9	July 23rd	Wolverhampton – London (Chiswick)	D. Sanderson	136	6.05.58

176

Circuit of Britain 1956

RACE RESULTS

GENERAL CLASSIFICATION

Position	Name	Time
1	R. McNeil – Nth East Counties	51.42.14
2	G. Taylor – Warwickshire	51.48.54
3	R. Killey – Merseyside	51.49.53
4	J. Rae – Scotland	51.53.00
5	F. Clements – Midland	51.57.47
6	D. Collins – Army C.U.	52.03.40
7	A. McPherson – Scotland	52.05.09
8	W. Shepherd – Nth W. Counties	52.21.01
9	J. Ryan – Merseyside	52.23.14
10	N. Purdy – Nth East Counties	52.25.12
11	B. Jackson – Manchester	52.34.38
12	N. Storey – Manchester	52.37.51

TEAM CLASSIFICATION

Position	Team	Time
1	N.E. Counties	157.04.50
2	Army C.U.	158.13.56
3	Greater London ..	159.23.10
4	South East	159.56.27
5	North West	160.40.29
6	Manchester	160.54.28

FACTS AND FIGURES	Total prize value £503
	Total distance 1,016 miles.
	Race average m.p.h 19.483
	45 finished

KING OF THE MOUNTAINS 13 PRIMES				
	1	J. Nicholson ..	..	25 points
	2	J. Ryan	.. ..	23 points
	3	G. Taylor	.. ..	22 points
	4	R. McNeil	.. ..	18 points
		T. Bristow	.. ..	18 points
	6	R. Killey	.. ..	15 points

STAGE RESULTS

Stage	Date	Route	Winner	Miles	Time
1	Aug. 11th	Skegness – Manchester	J. Rae	163	8.42.36
2	Aug. 12th	Manchester – Morecambe	P. Ward	131	7.01.20
3	Aug. 13th	Morecambe – Rhyl	F. Clements	115	5.53.29
4	Aug. 14th	Rhyl – Barmouth	5 riders declared FIRST	64	2.10.00
		Barmouth – Aberystwyth	R. Killey	58	6.37.50 (overall)
5	Aug. 15th	Aberystwyth – Barry	F. Clements	139	7.19.05
6	Aug. 16th	Barry – Weston-S-Mare	W. Shepherd	132	6.25.45
7	Aug. 17th	Weston-S-Mare – Lee on Solent	J. Grieves	129	5.43.25
8	Aug. 18th	Cosham – Midhurst TT	D. Collins	34	1.13.21
		Midhurst – Worthing	D. Collins	51	2.03.10

177

Index

Addie, 24, 34, 35, 36, 37
Albert, 105, 106, 108
Aldridge, 42, 58, 115
Allamic, 85, 87, 88
Amelynck, 82
Andrews, 101, 102, 103, 104, 106
   108
Armes, 115, 116, 117, 123
Armitage, 134, 139, 140, 142, 144,
   145
Armstrong, 151, 157
Audemard, 19, 20, 22, 23, 28, 30,
   31, 42
Auquier, 106

Baele, 63, 64, 65, 67, 69, 72, 73
Bailes, Viv, 71, 115, 116, 117, 118,
   119, 120, 122, 123, 124, 126,
   127, 128, 131, 133, 135, 138,
   140, 141, 145, 146
Baker, 119
Bamforth, 116
Bartrop, Dick, 101, 102, 103, 104,
   105, 108, 111, 112, 131, 132,
   134, 146
Baty, Bill, 133, 136
Baxter, 142
Bedwell, Dave, 20, 21, 22, 23, 24,
   25, 28, 29, 30, 31, 32, 33, 34,
   37, 62, 63, 64, 65, 66, 67, 69,
   70, 71, 72, 73, 74, 76, 77, 80,
   82, 84, 85, 88, 90, 91, 92, 93,
   94, 96, 97
Bellay, 61, 62, 63, 66, 67, 70
Bellamy, 25, 48, 49, 54, 55, 66
Bennett, 126, 127
Bentley, 119
Bezamet, 81, 84, 86, 87, 91, 92,
   96, 98
Bingham, 161

Birchall, 164, 166
Bladon, 141, 142
Blair, 28, 29, 42, 46, 53, 58
Blissett, 103, 111, 112, 139
Bloomfield, 28
Bodenham, 157, 160
Bodson, 57
Booker, 92, 93, 94, 106, 108, 111,
   112
Borcy, 105, 106
Bourgeois, 57
Bowes, 115
Boyd, Paddy, 130, 134, 135, 136,
   139, 140, 141, 142, 163, 164,
   165, 168
Brackstone, John, 40, 41, 42, 49,
   51, 136, 139
Bradley, Bill, 150, 152, 153, 154,
   155, 156
Bradshaw, 120
Bristow, 138, 144, 155, 156, 158,
   159, 161, 162, 165
Bronkaert, 81
Brooke, 115, 116
Brown, Ian, 108
Browne, Reg, 116, 117, 131, 133,
   136, 137, 138
Burford, 115, 116
Butlin, Billy, 99
Buttle, Derek, 20, 28, 29, 31, 32,
   33, 64, 71, 72, 87, 96

Carr, 53
Carroll, Frank, 115, 116, 119,
   120, 122, 131, 137, 140, 142,
   144
Chiti, 62, 63, 70, 73, 74, 75, 76
Christison, Joe, 51, 56, 57, 81,
   82, 87, 88, 101, 102, 104, 105
   110

179

Ciancola, 61, 62, 63, 64, 65
Ciolli, 63, 64, 65
Clark, G., 23, 25, 28, 29, 33
Clark, R., 162, 163
Clarke, D., 52, 72, 75, 77, 119
Clements, F., 152, 155, 156, 157, 158, 160, 162, 163, 164, 168
Collins, Doug, 152, 158, 163, 165, 167, 168
Collinson, 138
Cook, 57
Coombes, 120, 123, 124, 128
Corbusier, 81, 82, 92, 94
Corfield, 154, 160, 161
Crane, 155, 167, 168
Cubitt, 117

Dark, 167
Dorpe, Van, 101, 102, 105
Dooren, Van, 43, 46, 49, 54, 55
Dowell, 145, 146
Dowling, 138, 142
Downham, 115, 116, 128
Drei, 84
Drinkwater, 41, 43
Duffy, 116, 117
Dunphy, 119

Eastwood, 22, 33, 34, 35
Ellison, Phil, 142, 144, 145, 150, 157, 158, 160, 161
Endruweit, 123
Evans, Derek, 115, 119, 127, 128, 131, 132, 136, 137, 140, 144, 146
Evans, Frank, 116, 122

Faccioli, 86, 88, 90
Faille, 84, 85, 86, 92, 94
Fenwick, Trevor, 22, 53, 54, 55, 56, 61, 63, 66, 70, 72, 76, 78, 91, 94
Forneau, 102, 104, 106, 108, 110, 111, 112
Fraser, 51

Garnier, 27, 28, 36, 37
Garvey, Frank, 64, 66, 67, 74, 75, 115, 116, 119, 123
Geneste, 61, 63, 64, 66
Gestri, 62, 63, 64, 66
Gill, 105, 106, 108
Glendenning, 146
Godbeer, 120, 122, 123, 124
Goddard, 136, 139, 150
Goss, 152
Greenfield, 24, 27, 30, 31, 34, 37, 45, 47, 51, 54, 66, 70, 72, 73, 74, 80, 87, 88, 90, 92, 94, 95
Greaves, 116
Gregg, 119
Gregorini, 42, 45
Gregory, 130, 131
Grieves, J., 166
Grondelaers, 66, 77
Guldemont, Henri, 63, 64, 65, 66, 67, 69, 72, 74, 76, 81, 85, 86, 87, 88, 91, 92, 93, 94, 95, 97, 101, 102, 103, 105, 106, 108, 109, 111

Hadlington, 116, 118, 123
Hall, 161
Harbottle, 123, 124
Harrison, B., 162
Haskell, Brian, 106, 107, 110, 112, 115, 116, 119, 120, 122, 123, 126, 128, 131, 138, 139, 140, 146
Hawkins, 40, 46, 51
Hetherington, 116, 120
Hewson, Tony, 101, 105, 107, 111, 112, 116, 119, 120, 122, 123, 126, 128, 133, 138, 142
Hibell, 21
Hier, 120
Hinch, 101
Hoar, 105, 106, 109, 110
Hodgson, 123, 128
Holland, J., 154, 155
Holliday, Ray, 70, 76, 133, 134, 135, 136, 139, 144, 146

Hope, 116
Howarth, 19, 31, 32, 52, 115, 116
Humphrey, Vic, 113, 114, 118,
125, 126, 128, 129, 139, 143,
144, 147, 149, 153, 158
Hutton, 156

Ilsley, Arthur, 61, 63, 64, 67, 70,
73, 74, 75, 76, 80, 82, 84, 96,
102, 104

Jackson, Alan, 135, 136, 138, 139,
152, 153, 154, 155, 156, 166
Jackson, L., 86, 93
Jacob, 84, 85, 90, 92, 93
Johnson, 49, 50
Jomoux, 81, 93
Jones Stan, 42, 43, 45, 48, 51,
57, 58, 59, 74, 82, 87, 88, 92,
94, 97
Jowett, Ken, 23, 27, 28, 32, 34,
41, 43, 44, 61, 66, 82, 83, 90,
92, 102
Jowers, Ron, 61, 62, 64, 74, 76,
116, 117
Joy, Ken, 81, 82, 87, 90, 92, 95

Keenahan, 61, 120, 124, 142
Kennedy, John, 115, 131, 132,
134, 136, 137, 139, 140, 145,
146
Killey, 157, 158, 159, 163, 164
Kopitz, 43, 44
Krebs, Fred, 80, 81, 82, 83, 84,
86, 96

Lamb, 115
Laurent, 19, 24, 30, 31, 34, 35
Law, 152, 160
Lawton, Eddie, 60, 112
Lawton, Audrey, 112
Lee, 116, 119, 120, 123, 125, 126,
128
Lees, Ted, 126
Lennon, Joe, 24, 31, 32, 36, 37
Lewis, Gwyn, 160, 162

Mackin, Ray, 116, 119, 120, 122,
123, 124, 126
Maestri, 42
Maitland, Bob, 40, 42, 51, 52, 53,
54, 55, 56, 59, 60, 63, 66, 70,
71, 72, 76, 82, 84, 86, 87, 91,
92, 94, 95, 96, 97, 98, 101, 105
Manns, 122, 123, 128
Marr, 51
Martin, 21
Mather, Chas, 43, 51, 52, 54, 55,
152, 153, 154, 157, 158, 160,
162, 163, 164, 166
Mather, James, 154, 160, 162
Mathieu, 64, 66
Matthews, M., 126, 127, 128
Mattivi, 102, 104, 106, 108
McCarthy, 24, 31, 32, 34, 35
McNeil, Dick, 149, 151, 152, 154,
156, 158, 159, 161, 162, 164,
165, 166, 167, 168
McPherson, 152, 154, 155, 156,
157, 166
Meade, 51
Mercier, 80, 81, 83, 84, 85, 87,
90, 91, 94
Michaux, 52, 56, 58, 59
Midgley, 116, 117, 119
Milsom, 117, 118
Mitchell, Ken, 82, 83, 86, 87, 88,
92, 93, 101, 103, 104, 105, 108,
111, 112
Monti, 62, 63, 65, 66, 70, 71, 73,
74, 76, 77
Morrish, 44
Morris, John, 101, 105, 138, 140
Morris, J. (Cycle), 149, 167
Moxhet, 101, 102, 106

Nascimbene, 84
Neal, 138, 141, 142
Needham, 145
Newman, Alf, 42, 51, 52, 54, 56,
57, 58, 74, 76, 84, 85, 86, 92, 93
Nicholls, 28, 29, 31, 32, 37
Nicholson, 145, 152, 155, 161,
162, 163, 165, 168

Norton, 150, 152
Nowell, 123, 128
Nye, 165

O'Reilly, 46

Park, 132
Parker, Clive, 20, 27, 28, 30, 31,
  33, 63, 66, 69, 70, 72, 75, 76,
  80, 82, 83, 84, 86, 93, 94, 96
Parkin, 61, 62, 77
Peakall, Doug, 17, 18, 33, 99,
  100, 104
Penvose, Ed, 101, 102, 131, 132,
  133, 134, 135, 140, 142, 144
Perks, 138, 139, 140, 145, 146
Peters, Sylvia, 114
Petty, Doug, 64, 65, 70, 77, 102,
  103
Phillips, T., 33, 49, 57
Pierre, 19, 20, 21, 22, 23, 24, 31,
  35, 40, 44
Pinnington, Pat, 152, 155, 156,
  157, 159, 161, 162, 164, 167
Plassa, 80, 94
Pottier, John, 46, 48, 54, 55, 56,
  63, 66, 67, 69, 71, 72, 75, 76,
  77, 78, 81, 82, 83, 84, 90, 92,
  101, 102, 105, 108
Pound, 45
Prinoo, 160, 161
Proctor, Pete, 42, 43, 46, 51, 52,
  53, 54
Pryor, 82, 87, 91, 92
Pugi, 82, 85
Purdy, 156
Pusey, 108, 109

Rae, James, 150, 151, 152, 155,
  156, 159, 160
Reeves, 62, 64
Richards, 25
Richardson, 139, 156, 159, 161,
  164
Roberts, 160, 163
Robinson, Brian, 61, 64, 66, 72,

76, 77, 80, 81, 82, 83, 84, 85,
  90, 91, 92, 96, 97
Robinson, Dave, 51
Robinson, Des, 92, 105, 106, 108,
  125, 131, 132, 133, 135, 136,
  137, 139, 140, 141, 145, 146
Ross, 136
Routledge, 128
Rowland, 116
Rudd, 123
Russell, Ken, 23, 25, 27, 28, 29,
  41, 42, 44, 45, 46, 47, 48, 49,
  51, 54, 55, 56, 57, 58, 59, 60,
  64, 70, 81, 86, 91, 92, 93, 106
Russenburger, 104, 106
Ryan, John, 155, 156, 157, 158,
  160, 165, 167, 168

Sanchez, 43
Sanderson, 138, 139, 140, 145,
  146
Saunders, J., 156, 162, 163
Saunders, S., 63, 66
Saunders, Tom, 83
Saville, Jimmy, 19, 24, 32, 80,
  134, 146, 152
Scales, Les, 20, 25, 27, 33, 45,
  46, 47, 51, 53, 54, 56, 58, 59,
  60, 63, 71, 72, 75, 76, 78, 92,
  95, 101, 110
Seel, Frank, 23, 25, 28, 33, 75, 76
Seggar, 155, 156, 157, 165, 166
Shepherd, 135, 163, 164, 166
Short, John, 103, 104, 117, 122,
  123, 141, 142
Smit, de, 44
Smith, Alan, 163, 164, 166
Smith, Tony, 40, 49
Stallard, Percy, 17
Stark, 117, 118, 120, 122
Steel, Ian, 19, 22, 23, 25, 28, 29,
  30, 31, 32, 34, 35, 36, 37, 38, 40,
  45, 46, 48, 49, 51, 52, 54, 55,
  56, 57, 60, 63, 69, 82, 84, 92,
  93, 95, 101, 102, 103, 104, 106,
  108

Stokoe, 159
Stonex, 120, 123
Stratford, 102, 123, 133, 134, 139
Summers, 136
Swinney, 131, 132

Talbot, Dennis, 61, 67, 70, 74, 76, 81, 84, 87, 92, 94, 95, 101, 102, 106, 108, 111
Tamburlini, Eugene, 64, 81, 82, 84, 85, 86, 87, 88, 90, 91, 92, 94, 96, 98, 112
Tanswell, 142, 146
Taylor, Alec, 20, 25, 27, 28, 29, 32, 34, 35, 37, 81, 82, 90, 94, 95
Taylor, G. (Wales), 130, 142
Taylor, Gil (Birmingham), 133, 135, 142, 150, 152, 154, 155, 157, 158, 160, 162, 164, 167, 168
Taylor, Norman, 150, 151, 159, 161, 162, 163
Thackeray, June, 101
Thom, Bob, 115
Thomas, 'Tiny', 42, 43, 45, 46, 49, 51, 54, 57, 58, 60, 70, 71, 75, 76, 77
Thomson, 44, 49
Tognaccini, 82, 84
Turner, 123, 139
Tweddell, Dave, 133, 136, 138, 141, 145

Vermaelan, 103, 104, 105
Vines, Graham, 102, 103, 104, 105, 106

Wade, 81, 90
Waterfield, 103, 105, 120, 145
Watson, 152, 155
Ward, Frank, 157
Ward, Peter, 133, 150, 152, 154, 155, 156
Welch, Johnny, 24, 42, 53, 54, 57, 61, 70, 73, 74, 75, 84, 86, 90, 92, 93
Wellman, 28, 29
West, Len, 19, 31, 33, 34, 42, 47, 48
Whitaker, 155
White, 133
Wightman, 44
Wilkinson, 142
Wilson, Don, 21, 22, 25, 27, 33, 34, 42, 52, 56, 58, 70, 74, 75, 76, 82, 87
Wilson, Jim, 33, 34
Wilson, Les, 72, 73, 74, 77, 86, 94
Wilson, Syd, 70, 101, 102, 103
Wiltcher, 155, 164, 165, 168
Wisinsky, 61, 62, 69, 70, 74, 75, 77
Wood, Bev, 31, 33, 34, 48, 49, 52, 53, 60, 62, 63, 66, 74, 90
Woodhouse, 120
Worsley, 125, 128
Wren, E., 101, 106, 111, 112, 133
Wright, 52

Yeaman, Norman, 40, 42, 53, 54, 57, 62, 64, 70

Ziegler, 43, 44